ON THE
ANCIENT COINS AND MEASURES
OF
CEYLON

THE INTERNATIONAL NUMISMATA ORIENTALIA

ON THE ANCIENT COINS AND MEASURES OF CEYLON

WITH A DISCUSSION OF THE CEYLON DATE OF THE BUDDHA'S DEATH

T.W. RHYS DAVIDS

GYAN

Published by

Gyan Publishing House
5, Ansari Road
Daryaganj, New Delhi-110002
Phone: 011-47034999, 9811692060
E-mail: books@gyanbooks.com

Distribution Network
gyanbooks.com
India, USA, Canada, UK, Australia, France

ISBN : 978-81-212-3845-8 (PB)
First Published, London, 1877

2nd Impression 2020

Printed at: Gyan Press, Delhi.

On the
Ancient Coins and Measures of Ceylon
Author: T. W. Rhys Davids

THE INTERNATIONAL

NUMISMATA ORIENTALIA.

THE ADVANCED ARTICLES HAVE BEEN UNDERTAKEN BY THE FOLLOWING CONTRIBUTORS:

DR. H. BLOCHMANN. GENERAL A. CUNNINGHAM. SIR WALTER ELLIOT. PROF. JULIUS EUTING. DON PASCUAL DE GAYANGOS. PROFESSOR GREGORIEF. MR. F. W. MADDEN. SIR ARTHUR PHAYRE. MR. REGINALD S. POOLE. MR. STANLEY L. POOLE. M. F. DE SAULCY. M. H. SAUVAIRE. MR. EDWARD THOMAS.

ON THE ANCIENT COINS AND MEASURES OF CEYLON,

WITH A DISCUSSION OF THE CEYLON DATE OF THE BUDDHA'S DEATH.

BY

T. W. RHYS DAVIDS,

OF THE MIDDLE TEMPLE, BARRISTER-AT-LAW; LATE OF THE CEYLON CIVIL SERVICE.

LONDON:

TRÜBNER & CO., 57 AND 59, LUDGATE HILL.

1877.

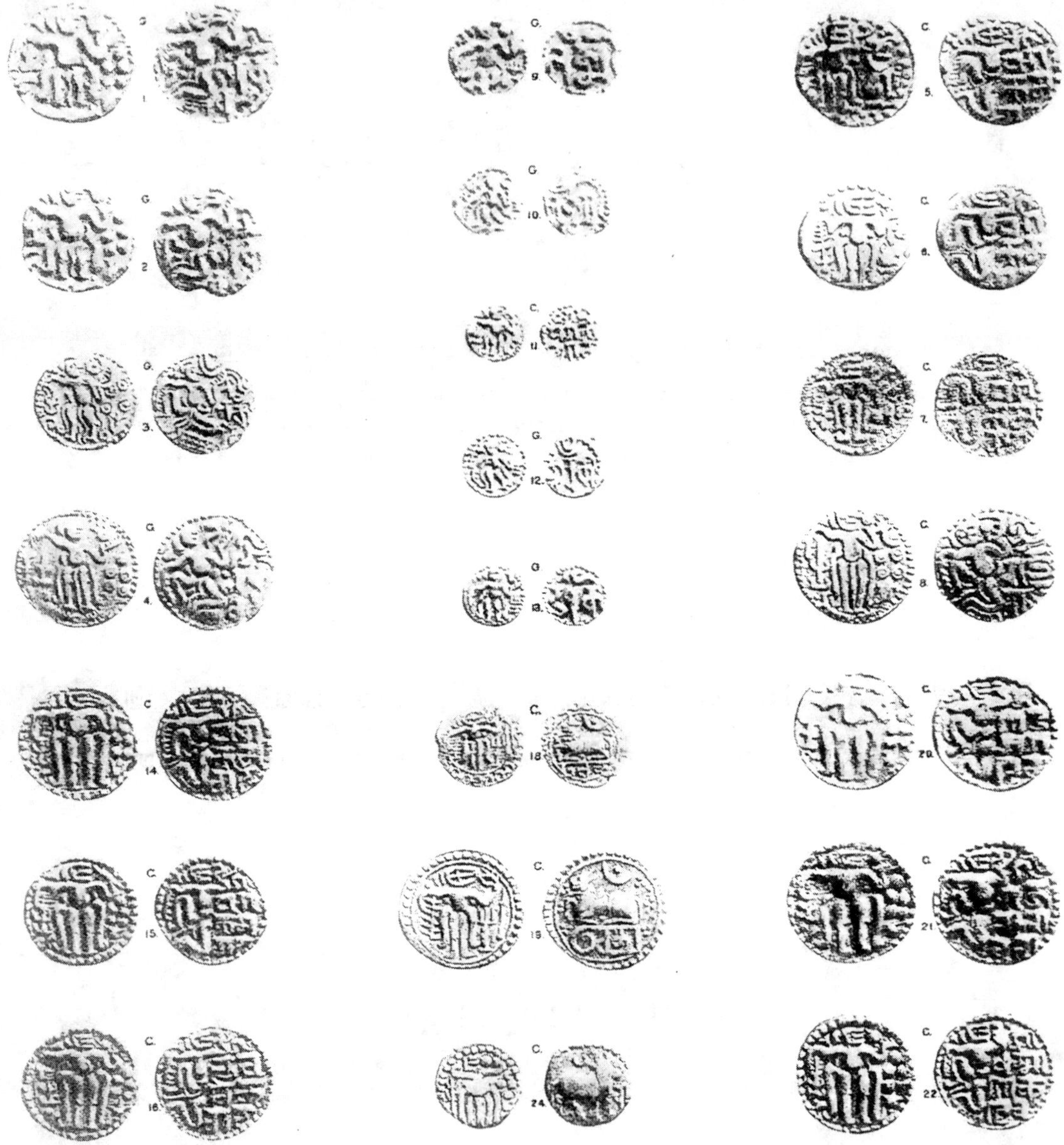

(For Index to the explanations see § 67.)

CONTENTS.

PART I.

REFERENCES TO COINS IN BUDDHIST LITERATURE

	SECTION
Introductory - - - - - - -	1, 2
Northern Buddhist Books - - - -	3
Southern Buddhist Books.	
1. Mahá Vagga and Kammavácá *(Páda)* -	4
2. Dhammapada *(Kahápaṇa)* - - -	5, 6
3. Khuddaka Páṭha - - - -	7
4. Párájika and Sutta Piṭaka (*Hiraññasuvaṇṇa*) - - - - - - -	8
5. Kaccáyana's Grammar - - -	9
6. Pátimokkha (*Rúpiya, kaṁsa*) - -	10–12
7. The Commentaries on do. (*másaka, kahápaṇa*) - - - - - - -	13
8. The Játakas - - - - -	14
9. The Commentary on do. (*sísa*) - -	15
10. Other Commentaries - - - -	16, 17
11. The Mahávaṁsa - - - - -	18
12. The Mahávaṁsa-Ṭíká - - -	19
13. Ceylon Inscriptions - - - -	20
Inference as to Ceylon coins from a passage in Pliny - - - - - - -	21
Summary of results - - - - - -	22

PART II.

WEIGHTS AND MEASURES.

Measures of Weight - - - - -	23, 24
Measures of Length - - - - -	25–30
The *Yojana* - - - - - -	27–29
Measures of Extent - - - - -	31
Measures of Capacity- - - - -	32–34

PART III.

SKETCH OF THE HISTORY OF CEYLON UNDER THOSE KINGS WHOSE COINS ARE EXTANT.

	SECTION
Introductory - - - - - - -	35
Wijaya Báhu I. - - - - - -	36
Parákrama Báhu the Great- - - -	37–39
Wijaya Báhu II. - - - - - -	40
Niṣṣanka Malla - - - - - - -	41
The times of trouble - - - - -	42
Wijaya Báhu III. - - - - - -	43
Paṇḍita Parákrama Báhu - - - -	44
Table of the Kings - - - - -	45

PART IV.

DESCRIPTION OF THE COINS.

Coins of Parákrama Báhu.	
1. The Lankeṣwara gold coin - -	46–48
2. The Lion coin - - - - - -	49
3. The half *massa* - - - - - -	50
4. The *massa* - - - - - - -	51
Coin of Wijaya Báhu II. - - - - -	52
,, Coḍaganga - - - - - -	53
,, Queen Líláwatí - - - - -	54
,, Sáhassa Malla - - - - -	55
,, Dharmáṣoka - - - - - -	56
,, Bhuwanaika Báhu - - - -	57
Doubtful Coins - - - - - - -	58–64
Coin of Rájarája - - - - - -	65
,, Niṣṣanka Malla - - - - -	66
References to the Plate - - - - -	67
Hook Money - - - - - - -	68–73

APPENDIX TO PART IV.

SECTION
European Ceylon Coins - - - - - 74–81

PART V.

THE CEYLON DATE OF GAUTAMA'S DEATH.

Northern and Southern dates of the Buddha's death - - - - - - - - - 82, 83
How far was the Ceylon date in actual use? 84–86
Authorities for the Ceylon date - - - - 87
The Ceylon date dependent on three data - 88
Date of Aṣoka's coronation - - - - 89–93
1. Date of Chandragupta's accession - 90
2. Aṣoka's Greek contemporaries - - 91, 92
Error in the Ceylon calculation of this period 94–97
The chronicles allow 218 years from Gautama to Aṣoka - - - - - - - - 98
SECTION
The Rája-paramparà.
1. Kings of Magadha - - - - 99, 100
2. Kings of Ceylon - - - - 101, 102
The Thera-paramparà - - - - 103–105
It allows only 150 years from Gautama to Aṣoka - - - - - - - - 106
This period more correct than the 218 years given in the books - - - - 107, 108
Suggested origin of the confusion - 109–118
The Ceylon and Purána lists of Magadha kings compared - - - - - - 110
Differences of one year - - - - - 114
Another Thera-paramparà - - - - 118
Is the shorter period correct? - - 119–121
Result - - - - - - - - - 122
How supported - - - - - - - 123
Summary - - - - - - - - 124

NOTE ON THE SAHASRÁM EDICT, p. 57.

Ruins of the JETAWANÁRÁMA, a Buddhist Temple at PULASTIPURA. (See § 37.)

ON THE ANCIENT COINS AND MEASURES OF CEYLON.

PART I. REFERENCES TO COINS IN BUDDHIST LITERATURE.

1. Ceylon and Kashmír are the only parts of India which pretend to possess a continuous native history. That of Ceylon is much the more ancient and complete, and as in it coins are not unfrequently mentioned, even in the earliest periods, it might have been supposed that some specimens of great age would have survived to our own days. Such is not however the case. We have at present only one series of coins of finished form and of a comparatively late date, beginning in the middle of the twelfth and ending at the close of the thirteenth century.[1] Our subject therefore divides itself naturally into two parts: in the first of which will be considered the data regarding coins and measures found in the Buddhist literature of Ceylon; while in the second those mediæval coins which have come down to us will be described and illustrated.

2. Mr. Thomas has already pointed out[2] how frequent are the allusions to money in the

[1] Just as I go to press I learn that there are some coins in the Colombo Museum with illegible inscriptions in square Páli characters. It would be interesting to learn whether they bear any of the signs, such as *j* or *s*, which have only as yet been found in Ceylon inscriptions. If not, they are probably importations from India.

[2] In his introductory essay to the Numismata Orientalia, 'Ancient Indian Weights,' p. 40.

sacred literature of the Buddhists; and as these occur in books of very different ages and authenticity, it will be necessary to quote and discuss the most important passages. Without a detailed examination of the passages themselves, we may easily be led to draw conclusions much too wide. Spence Hardy's statement,[1] for instance, that 'in the most ancient laws of the Buddhists the distinction is recognized between coined money and bullion,' is not confirmed by the texts hitherto accessible, unless the word 'coined' be taken in an unusually extended sense.

3. The time has scarcely arrived when anything can be affirmed with certainty as to the age of the different books of the Northern Buddhists: they show a state of belief much later and more developed than that of the Southern Church; but they claim a very high antiquity, and it is well known that amongst these ruder peoples the Buddhist mythology had a much more rapid development than that which took place in Magadha and in Ceylon. Buddhism became the State religion of the Indo-Skythians under Kanishka at about the beginning of our era, but no canon of the Northern Buddhists was settled at the council held under his auspices.[2] The books considered sacred by the Northern Church are mostly of much later date; but some of them were certainly translated into Chinese in the first century A.D.—that is, if reliance can be placed on the later native historians of China,[3] besides whose statements we have very slight data of any chronological value. Eugène Burnouf has given several instances of the mention of coins in those portions of the Northern Buddhist books he has translated,[4] and has discussed their values in a special note (p. 597). As all these works are of unknown authorship and date, but probably at least 700 years after our era,[5] the only conclusion to be drawn from these references is that they add simply nothing to our knowledge of the dates at which the coins mentioned in them were first used.

4. The canon of the Southern Buddhists was settled two centuries and a half earlier than the time of Kanishka, viz. under the Emperor Aṣoka in Páṭaliputra, about 250 B.C.; and it includes separate works by different authors.[6] The following passage occurs in the first chapter of the inedited Mahá Vagga in the Vinaya Pitaka, and also in the first chapter of the *Kammavácaṁ*, containing the liturgy used at the admission of laymen to the Buddhist order of mendicants, of which several translations and editions have already appeared.[7] (p. 6, line 4, of Mr. Dickson's edition of the Upasampadá-Kammavácá) 'If any mendicant takes a *páda* (*i.e.* a quarter), or anything

[1] Eastern Monachism, p. 66.

[2] Lassen, Indische Alterthumskunde, 2nd ed. vol. ii. p. 856. My 'Buddhism,' p. 239. 'Foe Koue Ki,' p. 248.

[3] Beal, Travels of Fa Hian, etc., pp. xx, et seq.; Romantic Legend of Sákya Buddha, p. vi.

[4] Thus the *suvarṇa* is spoken of in the Kanakavarṇa sútra and in the Púrna avadána (Burnouf, Introduction à l'histoire du Bouddhisme, pp. 91, 238, 243, 245); the *kárshápaṇa* in the Divya avadána (ibid, p. 147; compare Hodgson's Essays, 1874, p. 20) and in the Púrṇa avadána (ibid, pp. 236, 243, 258); the *purána* in the Divya avadána (ibid, p. 146); the *másaka* in the Púrṇa avadána (ibid, p. 243); the *kákaṇi* in the Aṣoka avadána, which is part of the Divya avadána (ibid, p. 392, and compare on the work itself Hodgson's Essays, 1874, p. 17); and lastly the *dínára* in this latter work and in the Hiranyapáṇi avadána (ibid, p. 432, note).

[5] Ibid, pp. 64, 231, 555; Weber's Sanskrit Literature, p. 262.

[6] This is clear from internal evidence: compare also James D'Alwis, *Buddhist Nirvana*, pp. 18, 19.

[7] The Padre Maria Percoto, Missionary in Ava and Pegu, translated it into Italian in 1776, and Professor Adler into German for the first volume of Egger's Deutsches gemeinnütziges Magazin, Leipzig, 1787. The Rev. Benj. Clough translated it into English in the second volume of the Miscellaneous Translations from Oriental Languages, London, 1834, and most of it was edited in Páli, with a Latin translation, by Professor Spiegel, Bonn, 1841. The best edition is that by Mr. Dickson in the J.R.A.S. for 1875, with English translation and notes.

of the value of a *páda* or more, he is *ipso facto* unfrocked.' Mr. Dickson translates *páda* 'the quarter of a pagoda,'[1] the pagoda being a small gold coin lately current in South India and worth 7*s.* 6*d.* Mr. Childers says in his Dictionary, 'There is a coin called pádo (Ab. 480): Subhúti quotes *poráṇa-kahápaṇassa catuttho bhágo pádo,* and states it is worth about sevenpence.' The Abhidhánappadípiká, to which the reference is given, was written in the twelfth century, and makes it the fourth part of a weight, apparently of the *nikkha,* which is made equal to five suvaṇṇas (§ 23 below). So that we have three modern authorities each giving a different meaning to the word. It is evident that they do not really know in what sense it was originally used, and there is nothing to prove that it meant a coin at all; it may have been a weight, either of gold, silver or copper, recognized as a basis of calculation or a medium of exchange.[2] All that can be said is that it was certainly of small value.

5. In the Dhammapada, a collection of ethical verses from other books of the Three Piṭakas, and one of the latest works included in the canon by Aṣoka's council, the word kahápaṇa is used in verse 186: *Na kahápaṇa-vassena titti kámesu vijjati,* 'Not by a rainfall of kahápaṇas will there be satisfaction in the midst of lusts.' The exact derivation and meaning of the word *kahápaṇa* is not quite so clear as one could wish. The corresponding Sanskrit word kárshápaṇa occurs already in Manu and Páṇini, of which the former is certainly, and the latter probably, earlier than the earliest possible date of the Dhammapada. It is clearly derived from karsha, the name of a small weight; but *paṇa,* which is usually supposed to be the second part of the compound, would not explain the second *á*, while the root *paṇ* 'to barter or bet,' is not used with the prefix *á* except in the nominal derivative *ápaṇa* 'market,' which does not help us much. In trying to determine the exact meaning from the texts, we are met with an ambiguity of expression which is only the reflexion of an ambiguity in idea; just as even in English the words 'coin' and 'money' are very vaguely used. Coin may, I think, be legitimately used in two senses; firstly, of pieces of metal bearing the stamp or mark of some person in authority as proof of their purity, and of their being of full weight; and secondly, of pieces similarly stamped, but thereby acquiring a value beyond that of an equal weight of metal (by the mark or stamp implying a promise to receive the coin at a higher than its intrinsic value). The latter, like our pennies and shillings, might be more appropriately termed tokens. Now there was a time in India, before coins in either of these senses were struck, when mere pieces of bullion without stamp at all, or merely with some private stamp, were used as money—that is, as a medium of exchange:[3] and the word kárshápaṇa, as used by the authors mentioned above, may mean either coins proper of the weight of a karsha, or only such pieces of metal of that weight. The latter was almost certainly its original meaning both in Sanskrit and Páli, and is, I think, the meaning in this verse of the Dhammapada. Buddhaghosha mentions[4] a gold and silver as well as the ordinary (that is, bronze or copper) kahápaṇa; and Professor Childers thinks that only gold pieces can be referred to in our

[1] Loc. cit. p. 13.

[2] Böhtlingk and Roth refer to a passage in the Ṣatapatha Bráhmaṇa where páda means the fourth of a certain gold weight; but to none where it means coin. They explain the change of meaning from 'a foot' to 'a quarter' through the idea of one leg being the fourth of a quadruped.

[3] Mr. Thomas, Ancient Indian Weights, p. 57.

[4] In the passage quoted below, § 13.

passage. But copper pieces will satisfy the requirements of every other passage, except one legendary one, where the word occurs;[1] and considering the much greater value of copper then than now, it is not so certain that we need even here take the word in any other than its ordinary sense. The value of the kahápaṇa changed of course with the varying value of copper, and even its weight may have varied a good deal; as much at least as different specimens of the fruit of the karsha (*Terminalia bellerica*) vary among themselves.[2] Its size and shape are uncertain; but this at least can be said, that the sculptor of the bas-reliefs at Bárahát[3] (who cannot have lived much more than a century later than the compiler of the Dhammapada) makes them square. Lastly, it should be mentioned that, according to Mr. Childers, the word kahápaṇa itself meant primarily a small *weight*,[4] and that our authorities differ hopelessly about the weight of the karsha: the Sanskrit authorities making it equal to *sixteen* máshas, each of which=2½ másakas=5 ratis; while Moggallána (§ 23) makes the akkha (which, teste Böhtlingk-Roth, is the same as the karsha)=2½ másakas=5 ratis (that is=*one* másha). On the former calculation Mr. Thomas makes the kárshápaṇa=to 140 grains, one of our current pennies weighing about 145 grains. M. Léon Fécr quotes a form gahápaṇa from the Játakas (Etude sur les Játakas, p. 102). The old form Karisápaṇa, mentioned by Moggallána (v. 481), has not yet been found in the texts.

6. There is a curious expression at Dhammapada, v. 108: 'Whatever sacrifice or offering a man may make here during a whole year in order to get merit, all of it is not worth *a quarter*.'[5] The commentator explains it 'to mean a quarter of the virtuous mind of one reverencing holy men.' This seems forced, but must be, I think, the real meaning of the words, taken in the connexion in which they stand.

7. The only other portion of the three Piṭakas published is the Khuddaka Páṭha, the shortest book in the Buddhist Bible, a selection of Buddhist hymns edited by Mr. Childers for the Journal of the Royal Asiatic Society, 1869. In it no mention is made of coins, but it is said that 'in the other world there will be no trafficking by means of gold.'[6] These two works would scarcely have been looked upon as sacred by the Council of Aṣoka held in B.C. 250, unless they had been composed some time before it. They may therefore be approximately placed at least as early as the end of the fourth century before Christ.

8. I cannot refrain from adding here a reference to a passage occurring in the Párájika of the first Piṭaka, and also in the Raṭṭhapála Sutta of the second Piṭaka, although the texts are not yet accessible. In the former we have an account of the manner in which a certain Sudinna

[1] They are all quoted in the following sections. The exception, a doubtful one, is referred to below, § 15. Játaka 94, 23, compared with 93, 22. Compare Thomas, *l.c.* p. 41, note 6.

[2] Mr. Thomas considers that this Myrobalan seed formed the basis upon which the old *Karsha* of 140 grains was framed. It constituted an article of extended commerce, in its dry state it was little subject to change, it was readily available in the Bázárs as a countercheck of other weights, and finally the ordinary weight accords closely with the required amount. Indeed selected specimens of desiccated seed from Bhilsa, now in the India Museum, weigh as high as 144 grains.

[3] Cunningham, Report of the Bengal As. Soc., quoted in Ancient Indian Weights, p. 59, note, compared with § 15 below.

[4] So also see Féer, Etude sur les Játakas, p. 102. Aud Colebrooke, Essays (ed. Cowell), vol. i. p. 531, says, 'A paṇa or kárshápaṇa is *a measure* of copper as well as of silver.'

[5] Fausböll, p. 34, sabbam pi taṁ na chatubhágam eti. Comp. p. 288 and the passage quoted by Prof. Max Müller in his note to v. 157.

[6] N'atthi hiraññena kayakkayaṁ, p. 11 of the separate edition. Prof. Childers translates 'no trafficking *for* gold,' but the instrumental case is doubtless used of the *medium* of exchange.

persuaded his parents to allow him to enter the Buddhist Order of Mendicants, and was afterwards tempted by them to return to a layman's life. In the latter a similar story, for the most part in the very same words, is told of Raṭṭhapála. In the translation of the former by the Rev. S. Coles we read that Sudinna's mother 'made two heaps for him, one of gold coins and the other of gold . . . . , and covered over those heaps with mats.'[1] In the translation of the latter by the Rev. D. J. Gogerly we read that Raṭṭhapála's father 'caused to be piled up a great heap of coined and uncoined gold, and covered it with a mat.'[2] The proffered wealth is in each case refused, the mendicant advising that 'the gold coins and the gold' (as Coles renders) or 'the gold and bullion' (as Gogerly here translates) should be thrown into the river. I have little doubt that the Páli words in all four passages are identical. Can they be the same as those used in the formula quoted by Burnouf as the standing mode of describing Gautama's own entry into the mendicant life? Burnouf quotes the passage from two Suttas of the second Piṭaka; and the words in question are simply *pabhútaṁ hiraññа-suvaṇṇaṁ*.[3] The first word, pabhúta, is either an archaic form of, or more probably a simple misreading for, the usual pahúta[4] 'much,' while each of the two parts of the following compound signifies 'gold.' That there was some shade of difference in the meaning of the two words is clear I think from the expression *hiraññaṁ vá suvaṇṇaṁ vá* 'either gold or gold,' in a commentary on the Pátimokkha,[5] but what the difference was when the second Piṭaka was composed is not so easy to say. Both words are constantly used both in Sanskrit and Páli in the simple sense of gold, both words also occur as names for a particular weight.[6] As names of weights the Suvaṇṇa according to Moggallána would seem to weigh forty Hiraññas, for it is equal to forty akkhas, an aksha is the same as a karsha, and hirañña at Játaka, p. 92, is replaced by kahápana at page 94.[7] But the usage of the fifth or twelfth century after Christ is poor evidence for the usage of the fourth century before Christ. It is quite possible that 'treasure and gold,' or 'gold and bullion,' or 'pounds of gold,' or 'yellow gold,' would be the right rendering of hirañña-suvaṇṇaṁ in the passages under consideration; but to decide these points we must have more texts before us. It will be of advantage, meanwhile, to have noted the similarity of the passages.

9. The date of the next work we have to consider is very uncertain. The orthodox Buddhists believe Kaccáyana's Grammar to be the work of a contemporary of Gautama: this is certainly incorrect, and even as late as the time of Buddhaghosha it was not acknowledged as the supreme authority on Páli grammar. The rules, explanations and examples are acknowledged by tradition to be by different hands, and the passage now to be quoted occurs among these later additions.[8] The Sinhalese tradition is, however, strong evidence that the work was composed in India and at a very early date—early, that is, as compared with the commentators

[1] Journal of the Ceylon As. Soc. 1876–1877, p. 187.

[2] Journal of the Ceylon As. Soc. 1847–1848, p. 95.

[3] Burnouf, Lotus de la bonne Loi, p. 863. Comp. Féer, Etude sur les Játakas, p. 107.

[4] *bh* and *h* can scarcely be distinguished in Ceylon MSS.

[5] Minayeff, p. 78, on Pátimokkha, ch. 8, v. 13.

[6] Hirañña is so used at Játaka 92, 22, Mah. 163, 2; Suvaṇṇa below (§ 23); and both the Suvaṇṇa and the Kárshápaṇa weighed 80 *ratis* according to Manu. Thomas, *loc. cit.* p. 13.

[7] So in Böhtlingk-Roth the hirañña is said to be = the karsha.

[8] On Kaccáyana's date see James D'Alwis in his 'Introduction' to Kaccáyana; Weber's review of this Introduction in Indische Streifen, vol. ii. pp. 316–343; and especially Burnell 'On the Aindra School of Sanskrit Grammarians,' 1875, pp. 61–62.

of the fifth century. At page 130 of M. Senart's excellent edition, under examples of the use of the ablative, occurs the curious expression: *satasmá* or *satena bandho naro*, 'a man bound for a hundred,' where one would expect baddho, and where the ablative is certainly strange. In a similar way, at Játaka 224, 24, we have *satena kítadáso*, 'a slave bought for a hundred.' Whether in these passages 'a hundred' means coins, or shells, or cattle, or weights of bullion, or corn, or other goods, is not certain, but I should take it to mean one hundred pieces of copper, *i.e.* kahápaṇas.[1] It will be seen hereafter that in the fifth century in Ceylon higher numerals were used in the same manner. Again, at p. 158, *upa nikkhe kahápaṇaṁ*, 'the kárshápaṇa is less than the nishka,' is given as an example of the use of the locative; here the grammarian who made the example was evidently thinking of weight, as the word nikkha is never in Páli used for a coin.[2] In Manu the weight of the nishka is 320 *ratis* in gold as against 80 ratis for the kárshápaṇa in copper.

10. We next come to the Pátimokkha, a compilation of unknown date, giving a classification, from the Vinaya Piṭaka, of offences against the rules of the Buddhist order of mendicants. It is certainly very old, but, not having been included in the canon by Aṣoka's Council, can scarcely have existed long before that time. A commentator of the fifth century[3] says indeed, according to Mr. Turnour's translation, 'Bhagawá (*i.e.* Gautama himself) taking his place in the midst of this assembly, held in the Weluwana edifice at Rájagaha, in the first year of his Buddhahood, ... propounded the Pátimokkham;' but it is impossible that the book so called should have come into existence until after the monastic system was worked out and settled in great detail, which it certainly was *not* at the time referred to. The same commentaries are used for the Pátimokkha and the Vinaya Pitaka, and the passages to be quoted probably occur also word for word in the latter. At verses 8, 9, and 10 of the sixth chapter [the Nisaggiya] *cívara-cetápanná* are mentioned, which Mr. Dickson translates 'money to buy robes.'[4] The origin of the expression is doubtful, Professor Childers ascribing the latter part of the compound to a confusion between the two roots *ci* and *cit*, and Mr. Minayeff, Mr. Dickson and one of the commentaries,[5] spelling the word cetápanna and making it masculine, while Professor Childers, another Páli commentary and M. Senart,[6] spell it cetápana, which makes it neuter. The former commentator explains it 'gold, or a pearl, or a jewel, or coral, or cotton cloth, or thread, or raw cotton,' that is to say, materials which could be made into a robe or bartered to procure one; the latter explains it simply 'price' or value (múla), but does not say in what. The term may therefore be rendered 'means to procure a set of robes,' and does not necessarily infer the existence of coined money.

[1] M. Senart translates 'pièces de monnaie,' but his attention was not directly drawn to this point. The curious may compare Judges xvii. 2, 3, 4, where 'hundreds' of silver are spoken of, and where the Authorized Version inserts the word 'shekels,' while some scholars would prefer to understand lambs.

[2] See below, § 23. Thomas, Anc. Ind. Weights, p. 13.

[3] The Madurattha-Vilásiní, Journal of the Bengal As. Soc. vol. vii. 1838, p. 816. A set of rules called Pátimokkha is five times mentioned in published parts of the Piṭakas (Dhammapada, verses 185, 375; Párájika, J. Ceylon As. Soc. 1867, p. 175; Sutta Nipáta, p. 95; and Sámañña-phala Sutta, Burnouf, Lotus, 463). But it is, to say the least, doubtful whether the book now known as Pátimokkha is referred to. Comp. Hardy, Manual, p. 198; Fausboll's Játaka, p. 85; Turnour in the J.B.A.S. vi. 519, 523; Beal, Catena, p. 189. That the word Pátimokkha was in use before the work so called assumed its present shape, is clear from the fact that the word occurs twice in the Pátimokkha itself. Dickson, p. 27.

[4] Page 47 of his separate edition from the Journal of the Royal Asiatic Society, 1875.

[5] P. 78 of Mr. Minayeff's edition, St. Petersburg, 1869.

[6] P. 322 of his separate edition of Kaccáyana.

11. Verses 18 and 19 say: 'If a priest receives or gets another to receive for him gold and silver [coin], or if he thinks to appropriate [money] entrusted to him, it is a nisaggiya fault. If a priest makes use of the various kinds of *money*, it is a nisaggiya fault.' I quote from Mr. Dickson's translation, but the words I have bracketed are not found in the original, and the word 'money' in the latter verse is in Páli *rúpiya*, which Professor Childers in his Dictionary translates *silver*, *bullion*. Neither the Páli *rúpiya*, nor the Sanskrit equivalent *rúpya*, are derived from rúpa in its sense of image, figure, or are ever used in the sense of 'bearing an image,' for which the correct expression is *rúpin*.[1] Silver is called *rúpiya* on account of its beauty, its shining appearance, just as gold is called *suvaṇṇa* on account of its fine colour. The commentator on this passage[2] explains *rúpiya* by *játarupa-rajata*, *gold and silver*, but this is rather a gloss on the *rule* than a philological explanation of the *word*. Moggallána distinctly confines the sense of the word to silver.[3] The text is as follows:—18. Yo pana bhikkhu játarúparajataṁ uggaṇheyya vá uggaṇhápeyya vá upanikkittaṁ vá sádiyeyya nisaggiyaṁ pácittiyaṁ. 19. Yo pana bhikkhu nánappakárakaṁ rúpiyasaṁvoháraṁ samápajeyya nisaggiyaṁ pácittiyaṁ.[4] I would translate: '18. If again a mendicant should receive *gold* or *silver*, or to get some one to receive it for him, or *allow it to be put in deposit for him*, it is a fault requiring restitution. 19. If again a mendicant should *engage in any of the various transactions in silver*, it is a fault requiring restitution,' where 'transactions in silver' must refer, I think, to the use of silver as a medium of exchange.

12. In the Bhikkhuní-Pátimokkhaṁ, or Rules for Nuns, occurs the passage, 'A nun collecting for a heavy cloak may collect as much as 4 kaṁsas; if she should collect beyond this, it is a fault requiring restitution. A nun collecting for a light cloak may collect as much as 2½ kaṁsas; if she should collect beyond this, it is a fault requiring restitution.'[5] There is some uncertainty as to the derivation and meaning of *kaṁsa*, which, as a measure of value, is only found in this passage. The word usually means copper, bronze, or a brass pot or plate; but the commentator[6] explains it here as 'four kahápaṇas,' an explanation found also in Moggallána's vocabulary.[7] In Sanskrit literature the word is only found in the sense of a brass pot or cup; but the Sanskrit lexicographers give kaṁsa as an equivalent of áḍhaka (a measure of capacity).[8] Mr. Childers regards it here as a derivative from, or a dialect variety of, karsha; but this seems indefensible, and the use in primitive times of a particular form of brass cup or plate as a measure of value is by no means unlikely, while the expression 'a bronze' is exactly paralleled by 'a copper' as used sometimes in English.[9] The tradition preserved in the Kankhá Vitaraní, that the weight of the kaṁsa, as a measure of value, was considered equal to four kahápaṇas, may or may not be well founded; one can only say that if the value were really so small, the idea of a cup or vessel can scarcely have been present to the mind of those who used the word.

[1] Páṇini perhaps thought differently. See the note in Anc. Ind. Weights, p. 39, but the passages quoted by Böhtlingk-Roth are conclusive.

[2] Minayeff, p. 80.

[3] Verses 486, 489, 903.

[4] Minayeff, p. 10. Dickson, p. 20.

[5] Minayeff, p. 103.

[6] Kankhá Vitaraní, ibid, p. 104.

[7] Abhidhánappadípiká, 905; he probably follows the fifth century commentary.

[8] Böhtlingk-Roth, s.v. Compare below, § 32, table; and Thomas, Anc. Ind. Weights, p. 26.

[9] Compare also the use of suvaṇṇa, § 23, and of ridi in Sinhalese.

13. In the commentaries written in Ceylon in the fifth century A.D. by Buddhaghosha, we find the following explanations. At page 66 of his edition of the Pátimokkha, Minayeff quotes a commentator's explanation of chora, a thief, as being one who takes anything of the value of five másakas[1] or more. Here the word másaka might just possibly mean a weight, but in the following passage that can scarcely be the case. The Kankhá-vitaraṇí on Pátimokkha vi. 10, quoted above, calls gold and silver and *kárshápaṇas* and *másakas* forbidden objects.[2] Another commentary on verse 18 says: 'By *rajata* (silver) is meant the kárshápaṇa, the metal másaka, the wooden másaka, the lacquer másaka, which are in use.'(!) And the Samanta-pásádiká on the same passage says:[3] '*játarúpa* is a name of suvaṇṇa (gold), which is also called satthuvaṇṇa because it is like the colour of Gautama Buddha,'(!) and after explaining *rajata* (which explanation Minayeff has left out in his edition, perhaps because it is the same as that given above), goes on: 'In this passage kahápaṇa is either that made of gold or that made of silver (*rúpiya*), or the ordinary one; the metal másaka means that made of copper, brass, etc.; the wooden másaka means that made of sára wood or of the outside of the bambu, or lastly of palmyra leaf, on which a figure has been cut (*rúpaṁ chinditvá kata-másako*); the lacquer másaka means that made of lac or gum, on which a figure has been caused to rise up' (*rúpaṁ samuṭṭhápetvá kata-másako*). Then, after explaining the words 'which are in use,' it continues: 'Lastly, every kind should be included, whether made of bone, or skin, or the fruits or seeds of trees, and whether with a raised image or without one.' It adds that the four forbidden things are silver, gold, the gold másaka, and the silver másaka, a different explanation from that given above. The annexed cut of a lacquer medal in the possession of Col. Pearse, R.A., may perhaps represent such a lacquer másaka as has just been referred to.

14. We next come to the Játakas, the date of the present text of which is very uncertain. It seems that a collection of Játaka stories was one of the earliest Buddhist books, and was included in the canon as settled by the Pátaliputra Council under Aṣoka; but it is the only book of that canon which has not been handed down to us in a shape purporting to be identical

[1] The másaka is the seed of a bean (see Thomas, loc. cit. p. 11), and is used in this sense at Mah. 239, 3. In Hardy's Legends and Theories of the Buddhists, sages are mentioned who 'had no cattle, no gold (not even as much as four másas, each of which is of the weight of six mára seeds) and no grain.' See below, § 23.

[2] Minayeff's Pát. p. 79. Comp. end of this paragraph.

[3] Ibid, p. 80. The full text is as follows:—*Játarúparajatan ti: játarúpaṁ náma suvaṇṇassa námaṁ, taṁ pana yassá Tathágatassa vaṇṇasadisaṁ hoti tassá Satthuvaṇṇo vuccatíti padabhájane vuttaṁ . . . . Tattha kahápaṇo ti: suvaṇṇamayo vá rúpiyamayo vá pákatiko vá. Lohamásako ti: tambalohádíhi katamásako. Dárumásako ti: sáradáruná vá velupesikáya vá antamaso tálapaṇṇena pi rúpaṁ chinditvá katamásako. Jatumásako ti: lákháya vá niyyásena vá rúpaṁ samuṭṭhápetvá katamásako. Ye voháraṁ gacchantíti: iminá pana pádena yo yo yattha yattha janapade yadá yadá vohāram gacchati. Antimaso aṭṭhimayo pi cammamayo pi rukkhaphalabíjamayo pi samuṭṭhápitarúpo asamuṭṭhápitarúpo sabbo pi saṁgahetabbo.* The greater part is given by Mr. Thomas *loc. cit.* p. 42, note.

with that accepted by the Council. The text exists now only in the commentary, the date of which is itself unknown, though it was certainly written in Ceylon, and probably as late as the fifth century after Christ. No kind of literature is more susceptible of verbal alteration than the easy prose narrative which forms the bulk of these tales; so that, although the text is throughout kept distinct from the commentary, it cannot be depended upon as an accurate reproduction of the original form. And again, though the mention of *money* is so mixed up with the gist of some of the stories that it can scarcely be due in those cases to interpolation, and may very possibly date from the first invention of the stories in the time of Buddha, or even earlier, the names mentioned may have been inserted afterwards. The Páli version of the Játakás is now being published by Mr. Fausböll; and the first part, containing the Páli text of the Introduction and of 38 Játaka stories, has already appeared in Copenhagen. In these stories are the following notices of money. In the Seri-váṇija Játaka[1] some poor people ask a hawker to take an old pot in exchange for his wares. The pot was gold, but so old and dirty that they did not know it. The hawker sees their foolishness, and hoping to get it for nothing, says it is not worth even half a *másaka*, and throwing it on the ground, goes away. Immediately afterwards another hawker comes up, and being made a similar offer, honestly tells the ignorant owners that their old pot is worth 'a hundred thousand' (sata-sahassaṁ),[2] but gives them for it 500 *kahápaṇas* and goods 'worth 500' (probably kahápaṇas). He then takes back eight kahápaṇas, and giving them to the captain of a vessel just then sailing, he escapes with the pot. The other hawker soon returns, and offers something of small value for the pot, and when its owners tell him they have given it to another hawker for 'a thousand' (sahassaṁ), he vainly pursues him, and then dies of grief and chagrin. The good hawker in this tale is the future Buddha; and had it been altered, the fact that he gave less than 'a thousand' for what was worth 'a hundred thousand' might have been easily got over by some interpolation; in any case the mention of money forms so important a part of the story that it must belong to a very early form of this Játaka.

The next mention of money is in the Cullaka-seṭṭhi Játaka.[3] On the advice of the future Buddha, a man earns 16 kahápaṇas in one day by the sale of firewood, and afterwards sells grass to the king's stable-keeper for 'a thousand,' and subsequently acquires a capital of 'a hundred thousand,' and marries the future Buddha's daughter.

In the Nandi-vásala Játaka[4] we have the history of a prize ox who first loses a bet (abbhutaṁ) of 'a thousand' for his owner, when the latter calls him vicious; and then wins a wager of 2000 when he calls him gentle; and in the next story the future Buddha, again under the form of an ox, wins for his mistress a bag containing 1000,[5] being hire for drawing 500 carts at two kahápaṇas a cart.

[1] Fausböll's Játaka, p. 111.

[2] At pages 69, line 15, and 178, line 21, other gold pots are mentioned worth 100,000 each.

[3] Fausböll's Játaka, p. 121.

[4] Ibid, p. 191.

[5] Sahassatthavika, J. 195, 20, compare 54, 1, and 55, 23. See on a parallel expression in the Rig-Veda, Mr. Thomas, Anc. Ind. Weights, p. 33.

15. Mr. Fausböll has also published from time to time 27 other Játaka stories,[1] but in these no mention is made of money. I pass on therefore to the commentary itself, in which the above stories are included. It commences with a short history of previous Buddhas, and then gives a succinct biography of Gautama Buddha. In the former a rich man says of his ancestors, 'when they went to the other world, they did not take with them even one kahápaṇa;' and *kahápaṇas* and leaden pieces (*sísa*) are mentioned among other kinds of wealth.[2] In the latter it is said that Vessantara's mother gave him at his birth a purse containing 1000, and Nalaka is said to have been born in a family worth 87 koṭis.[3] Buddha[4] gives Kiságotamí a necklace 'worth a hundred thousand,' and Anáthapiṇḍika is said to have paid 18 koṭis of gold (!) for the ground on which he built, at a further cost of 18 koṭis, the Jetavana, the first Buddhist monastery.[5] It is noteworthy that the only mention of gold kahápaṇas should be in this late version of an early legend, and in the commentator referred to above (§ 13).

16. In Buddhaghosha's commentary on the Saṅyutta Nikáya, written in the early part of the fifth century, king Kappina, a contemporary of Buddha, is said to have given 1000 to certain merchants;[6] and in his commentary on the Dhammapada (Fausböll, p. 333, and comp. p. 235) he contrasts a 'thousand' with a kákaṇiká, which is the same as the gunjá (below, § 23).

17. In another of Buddhaghosha's commentaries is the following passage: 'On that occasion the bhikkhus (mendicants) of Wesáli, natives of Wajji, on the Uposatha (Sabbath) day in question, filling a golden basin with water and placing it in the midst of the assembled mendicants, thus appealed to the upásakas (lay disciples) of Wesáli who attended there: 'Beloved, bestow on the order either a *kahápaṇa* or a half, or a quarter of one, or even the value of a *mása.*'[7] It would seem from this passage that Buddhaghosha considered the *mása* as less than a quarter of the value of the kahápaṇa, and *mása,* which form has not yet been found elsewhere, is, I suppose, the same as *másaka.* It should be noticed that the sentence occurs in a description of the Second Council 100 years after Gautama's death, which council, some think there is reason to believe, never actually took place; and that the Mahávansa, describing the same event, only mentions kahápaṇas. But that there was some such heresy there can be little doubt, as Aṣoka in the eighth Girnar edict talks of honouring Theras with gold.[8]

18. In this passage of the Mahávansa, which is a little later, 'gold and other coins'[8] are mentioned in Turnour's translation as one of the exceptions which the Wajjian heretics allowed themselves, only 100 years after the Teacher's death, to his comprehensive rule that the members

[1] For the names and dates of these publications see my 'Report on Pali and Sinhalese,' at p. 64 of the Annual Address of the President to the Philological Society for 1875.

[2] Játaka, p. 2, line 25; p. 7 line 3 from end; and p. 33.

[3] Játaka, 55, 18.

[4] Játaka, p. 61, line 10.

[5] Játaka, p. 92, ll. 22, 26. At p. 94, l. 23, it is said that the ground was bought by covering it with kahápaṇas laid side by side. Compare above, § 5, and Childers' Dict. p. ix.

[6] Sahassaṁ: apud d'Alwis, Introduction to Kaccáyana's Grammar, p. 97.

[7] Turnour, J.B.A.S. vol. vi. p. 729. Mr. Thomas has pointed out this passage, Anc. Ind. Weights, p. 41, but it is not, as there stated, from the Mahávansa. The golden basin should be, I think, a bronze dish (kaṁsapáti). Comp. Mah. 15, last line.

[8] Mahávansa, Turnour's edition, p. 15, line 10. The Páli word is játarúpádikaṁ. Lassen, Indische Alterthumskunde, vol. ii. p. 84 (first edition); Köppen, Religion des Buddha, vol. i. p. 147; and Cunningham, Bhilsa Topes, p. 78, who all mention *coins*, derive their information from Turnour. With this notice the passage in Aṣoka's edicts should be compared, where he mentions the honouring of 'Theras' with gold as a virtuous act. (thairáṇaṁ hiraṇapaṭividhánaṁ. Bombay Journ. 1843, p. 257; J.R.A.S. xii. 199; Burnouf, Lotus, 757; Kern, Jaartelling, 58).

of his order were not to receive gold or silver; but the original has simply 'gold, etc.,' though immediately afterwards it states that the mendicants even went so far as to call upon the laity to give them 'kahápaṇas.'

Further on in the Mahávansa a brahmin named Pandula gives Chitta's son 100,000;[1] King Dushṭa Gámaṇi (B.C. 161–137) gives a soldier 1000, and afterwards 10,000;[2] Wasabha, a nobleman in Dushṭa Gámaṇi's reign, gives another soldier 10,000;[3] Dushṭa Gámaṇi rewards a famous archer with a heap of kahápaṇas large enough to bury his arrow;[4] and when he builds the Maricawaṭṭi dágaba he makes presents valued at 100,000 and 1000, and spends altogether on that spot 19 koṭis, on the Brazen Palace 30 koṭis, on the Ruwanwæli Dágaba 1000 koṭis, and 100,000 on the sacred Bo-tree.[5] The same king rewards the architect of the Maháthúpa (now called the Ruwanwæli Dágaba) with a suit of clothes worth 1000, a splendid pair of slippers and 12,000 kárshápaṇas, and deposits 16 laks of kárshápaṇas for the workmen's wages.[6] He had previously deposited 32 laks of *hiraññas* for the wages of the workmen at the Lohaprásáda,[7] and he afterwards sends to a monk at Píyangala, among other things, two robes worth 1000, and the monk accepts them.[8] Dushṭa Gámaṇi's successor, Sardhá Tishya (B.C. 137–119), is said to have rebuilt the Brazen Palace at a cost of nine laks,[9] and his son and successor spent four laks for similar purposes.[10] King Mahánága, surnamed the Large-toothed (A.D. 9), spent six laks on the monks,[11] and the wife of the prime minister of Subha (A.D. 60) gives a youth named Vasabha 1000,[12] and he becoming king presents 1000 to the Mahávihára monastery, and land worth a lak to Abhayagiri, and his queen pays a lak for land on which to build another.[13] King Tissa (A.D. 209) gives 1000 monthly to the monks, and his successor gives them cloth of the value of two laks.[14] King Sangha Tissa (A.D. 242) put four gems worth a lak on the summit of the Ruwanwæli Dágaba,[15] and Jeṭṭha Tissa spent 16 millions on the Brazen Palace.[16] Under the reign of Mahasena (A.D. 284) occurs the phrase 'liable to a fine of a hundred';[17] and also the remarkable statement that that king gave to a thousand monks a theraváda worth 1000.[18] Meghavarṇa spends a lak in honour of the arrival of the Tooth-relic about A.D. 310.[19] Finally Dhatusena (A.D. 459)—in whose reign Mahánáma, the author of the Mahávansa, wrote—is recorded to have given 1000 in order to make the Dípavansa public,[20] and to have spent a lak on the sacred Bo-tree.[21]

19. Lastly, in the Mahávansa Tíká, a commentary on the Mahávansa written by the author himself, occurs the curious passage pointed out by Mr. Thomas,[22] where it is said that Chánakya, afterwards the minister of Chandra-gupta, but then, *circa* B.C. 330, a private individual, 'converted

[1] Páli sata-sahassaṁ, Mah. p. 61.

[2] Páli sahassaṁ and dasa-sahassaṁ, Mah. p. 139; 10, 11, 14. 140; 1, 3, 4. Dushṭa Gámaṇi is probably antedated about half a century, but this is of very little importance for our purpose.

[3] Dasasahassaṁ, Mah. 142, 9.

[4] Kahápaṇehi kaṇḍaṁ taṁ ásitto uparúpari
Chádápetvána dápesi Phussadevassa taṁ khaṇe.
—Mah. 157, 6.

[5] Mah. 160, 13; 161, 2; 165, 2, 6; 195, 8.

[6] Mah. 175, 7, 11.

[7] Mah. 163, 2.

[8] Mah. 177, 5.

[9] Mah. 200, 10.

[10] Mah. 201, 202.

[11] Mah. 214, 10.

[12] Mah. 219, 12.

[13] Mah. 223, 10, 14.

[14] Mah. 228, 6.

[15] Mah. 229, 4.

[16] Mah. 233, 10, 11.

[17] Mah. 234, 13 (Sataṁ daṇḍiyo).

[18] Mah. 237, 11. Comp. Childers' Dict. s.v. váda.

[19] Mah. 241, 13.

[20] Mah. 257, 14.

[21] Mah. 258, 10.

[22] Anc. Ind. Weights, p. 41; Turnour's Mahávansa, p. xl.

(by recoining) each kahápaṇa into eight, and thus amassed 80 koṭis of kahápaṇas.' As all statements by Mahánáma regarding this early period must be used with the greatest caution, the passage can only be received as evidence, not of what Chánakya did, but of what Mahánáma thought likely. Even so, it is very striking. In the passage referred to on the next page (p. xli), it is probable that the Páli original for Turnour's expression 'a thousand kahápanas' was simply sahassaṁ, 'a thousand,' just as a koṭi and a lak are mentioned at the top of page xl.

20. Such works as were produced in Ceylon between the fifth and the twelfth century have been so far lost that no book now extant can be assigned with certainty to that period; but in a very ancient inscription at Mihintale, of which I made a copy, mention is made of an aka, *i.e.* aksha, of gold (the aksha being the same as the karsha), and of the kalanda, which is the same as the dharana, and equal to eight akas.[1] The inscription records a lengthy order made by King Siri Sang Bo for the regulation of the Temple property at Mihintale. There were several kings of that title, and the inscription is ascribed by Dr. Goldschmidt to Mahindu III. (A.D. 1012).

21. In addition to these notices from Ceylon literature, a passage of Pliny should be mentioned, where it is stated that a traveller in the reign of Claudius was carried over to Ceylon from the Persian Gulf by unfavourable winds. The King of the place where he landed, and which he calls Hippuros, seeing some of his Roman coins, was astonished that the denarii should weigh the same, although the different figures upon them showed that they were struck by different persons.[2] It is very doubtful where Hippuros may be; possibly it was in the north of the island, and the King would then be the Tamil ruler over those parts, the province of Jaffna having been at that time, and for long afterwards, an independent, though perhaps tributary State. If the exact motive for the King's astonishment has been accurately preserved in this very secondary evidence, the negative conclusion might be drawn that the art of coining was very little advanced about the commencement of our era in the neighbourhood of Hippuros; and perhaps the positive one that the people thereabouts used pieces of copper of unequal weights, and with various marks upon them, as a medium of exchange. This is not inconsistent with the notices in the Ceylon books, and may therefore be taken as confirmatory evidence; but much stress cannot be laid upon it, as our informant may have been misled. The motives of Indian rájas are by no means easily ascertained, even when they are speaking to people who understand their language. And the other details stated by Pliny are so evidently incorrect—he says, for instance, that the King's palace alone contained 200,000 people—that no reliance can be placed on the accuracy of his report.

[1] Clough says the kalanda is the weight of 24 mára seeds = 86 grains and a fraction.

[2] Pliny, Nat. Hist. vi. 24. Mirum in modum in auditis justitiam ille suspexit, quod pares pondere denarii essent in captivâ pecuniâ cum diversæ imagines indicarent a pluribus factos. Compare Lassen, Ind. Alt. vol. iii. p. 61; Priaulx, Indian Embassies to Rome, J.R.A.S. vol. xviii. p. 345. Prof. Lassen would identify Hippuros with Kudirei Malei, on the N.W. coast, a place Sinhalese at the time referred to, but whose present Tamil name means Horse Hill; Bochart identifies it (Geogr. Sacr. vol. i. p. 46) with Ophir, which Gen. Cunningham places at the mouth of the Indus (Ancient Geog. India, vol. i. p. 561); and Sir E. Tennent, for much less valid reasons, at Galle in Ceylon (vol. ii. p. 101). Of these I would prefer Lassen's opinion; for though Kudirei Malei may be a modern name, it may also be a translation of a more ancient one. But the point is as yet quite uncertain.

22. We have thus derived enough data from the few fragments of Buddhist literature as yet published to render the hope reasonable that we shall hereafter, when the whole of it has become accessible, be able to decide most of the points at present doubtful regarding the coinage of Magadha in the time of the Piṭakas, and of Ceylon in the fifth century. At present we can only sum up as follows the facts ascertained and the conclusions deducible from them.

In the Northern Buddhist literature coins have only as yet been found mentioned in works of uncertain but very late date (§ 3). In the Southern Buddhist literature we have the *kahápaṇa* and the *páda*, i.e. 'quarter,' distinctly used in the Piṭakas themselves—though each only in one passage—as measures of value (§ 4, 5), and buying and selling by means of gold is mentioned (§ 7). In Kaccáyana's Grammar the word *kahápaṇa* is once used, apparently as the name of a weight; and the expression, 'bound for a hundred,' implies the existence of some well-known measure of value, which probably, though not conclusively, was the *kahápaṇa* (§ 9). In the Pátimokkha, besides a reference to transactions in which gold and silver are concerned (§ 11), we have the distinct mention of the *kaṁsa* or 'copper' as a measure of value (§ 12). In the fifth century commentaries we find the words *kahápaṇa* and *másaka*[1] (which originally meant a weight) explained as names for pieces of money on which images or figures were stamped or marked. Both are used in the Játakas and *sísa*, leaden piece, in the Játaka commentary, where *kahápaṇa* is used in a passage referring to the time of Gautama (§ 13–17). In the earlier portions of Mahánáma's history, where many of the statements are not trustworthy, the *kahápana* and *hiraññа* are mentioned, and throughout his work there are references to a 'hundred,' a 'thousand,' a 'ten thousand,' a lak, and a koṭi (ten million), as if these were recognized weights or sums (§ 18). In the commentary on the same work similar expressions are used, and we are told that a private individual, converting each kahápaṇa into eight, amassed eighty koṭis (§ 19). We have, therefore, no evidence in Buddhist literature that in Magadha before the time of Aṣoka, or in Ceylon before the fifth century A.D., there were any coins proper, that is, pieces of inscribed money struck by authority. On the other hand we have no statements inconsistent with the existence of such coinage; and we have sufficient evidence that pieces of metal of certain weights, and probably marked or stamped by the persons who made them, were used as a medium of exchange; and that some common forms of this money had acquired recognized names. These results are substantially in accordance with the general course of Mr. Thomas's argument (*loc. cit.* pp. 32-44). 'True coins in our modern sense'[2] are not mentioned in any Indian work certainly pre-Buddhistic, but 'circulating monetary weights'[3] were in use long before. The oldest coins found in India, whose dates can be even approximately ascertained, are not older than the first century B.C., and were almost certainly struck in imitation of the Greeks.[4] Into the general question, however, I do not enter: my object has been a much humbler one, viz. to state clearly such evidence as to coins or money as is obtainable from the published Páli texts.

[1] Once called mása (§ 17). [2] Mr. Thomas, Ancient Indian Weights, p. 41. [3] Ibid. p. 36.
[4] But compare Mr. Thomas contra, Prinsep's Essays, vol. i. p. 222.

PART II. Weights and Measures.

23. We shall group our notices of these in the form of a commentary on the statements of Moggallána, who, in the middle of the twelfth century, composed a Páli vocabulary called Abhidhánappadípiká, in imitation of the Amara Koṣa. In this work he gives various schemes of measures,[1] which contain valuable information, although it will, I think, be clear from the following pages that his tables cannot be entirely relied on as evidence of Indian or even of Ceylon usage. As it refers to the points we have just been discussing, we place first his

TABLE OF WEIGHTS.

2 Gunjá[2] =	1 Másaka[3] (a seed of the *Phaseolus*).							
5 do. =	**2½** do. =	1 Akkha (a seed of the *Terminalia Bellerica*) = karsha.						
40 do. =	20 do. =	**8** do. =	1 Dharana (= Sinhalese kalanda).					
200 do. =	100 do. =	40 do. =	**5** do. =	1 Suvaṇṇa (gold).				
1,000 do. =	500 do. =	200 do. =	25 do. =	**5** do. =	1 Nikkha (an ornament for the neck).[4]			
400 do. =	200 do. =	80 do. =	**10** do. =	2 do. =	½ do. =	1 Phala (fruit).		
40,000 do. =	20,000 do. =	8,000 do. =	1,000 do. =	200 do. =	50 do. =	**100** do. =	1 Tulá (scale).	
800,000 do. =	400,000 do. =	160,000 do. =	20,000 do. =	4,000 do. =	1,000 do. =	2,000 do. =	**20** do. =	1 Bhára (load).

24. The thick-faced figures are the ones given by Moggallána, the others being calculated from them. On careful inspection it will be seen that we have here at least two tables, and the connexion between the two, which Moggallána establishes by making one phala=10 dharanas,[5] is probably fictitious; for as far as Nikkha the weights are applicable to substances of great value and small bulk, and the rest *vice versâ* to things of small value and greater bulk. It is incredible that hay and gold should have been measured by one scale. None of these words are used in the published Páli texts in the sense of definite weights, except perhaps phala (mention being made in the commentary on the Pátimokkha[6] of a phala of coral) and másaka, which word has been discussed above. The gunjá is another name for the rati, on which see Mr. Thomas's paper, p. 10–11. The whole of this table should be compared with those given by the Sanskrit authorities,[7] and by the Amara Kosha (Colebrooke, p. 241), from which it varies almost throughout. It is curious that Moggallána does not mention in the table the only measure of weight actually found in use, viz. the *Káca* or *Kája*, a pingo-load: that is, as much as a man can carry in two baskets suspended from a pole carried across his shoulders.[8]

[1] Verses 267–269, 194–187, 479–484.

[2] A seed of the *Abrus precatorius* = kákaṇiká, § 16.

[3] Hardy, Legends and Theories of the Buddhists, p. 4, speaks of Rishis who had 'no gold (not even as much as 4 massas, each of which is of the weight of 4 mára seeds),' but what plant is meant by mára does not appear either in Clough's or in the Petersburg Dictionary. Comp. above § 5 (at the end) and § 17.

[4] So used at Dhp., pp. 41, 367. Comp. Anc. Ind. W. p. 34.

[5] It is curious that in Manu's table, on the contrary, 10 phalas = one Dharana. See Anc. Ind. Weights. p. 20, note 4.

[6] Minayeff, p. 79, note on 8, 13; but the masculine gender is used, which Childers gives only in the sense of fruit. Moggallána makes the weight neuter.

[7] Colebrooke, Amara Kosa, p. 241, and Essays (ed. Cowell), pp. 529–532. Thomas, *loc. cit.* p. 13.

[8] Mah. 22, 27; Játaka, 9, 17; Ab. 525, 919.

25. We pass on to Moggallána's scheme of the

MEASURES OF LENGTH.

36	Paramáṇus	=1 Anu.						
36	Aṇus	=1 Tajjári.						
36	Tajjáris	=1 Rathareṇu.						
36	Rathareṇus	=1 Likkhá.						
7	Likkhás	=1 Uká.						
7	Ukás	=1 Dhaññamása.						
7	Dhaññamásas	=1 Angula[1] (finger joint, inch).						
12	Angulas	= 1 Vidatthi (span).						
24	do.	= **2**	do. = 1 Ratana (cubit, forearm) = hattha[2] = kukku.					
168	do.	= 14	do. = **7**	do. = 1 Yaṭṭhi (pole, walking stick).				
[672	do.	= 56	do. = **28**	do. = 4	do. = 1 Abbhantara (interval)].[3]			
3,360	do.	= 280	do. = 140	do. = **20**	do. = 5	do. = 1 Usabha.[4]		
268,800	do.	=22,400	do. =11,200	do. =1,600	do. = 400	do. = **80**	do. = 8 Gávuta (meadow).	
1,075,200	do.	=89,600	do. =44,800	do. =6,400	do. =1,600	do. =320	do. = **4**	do. =1 Yojana.

Also at verses 197, 811, a *kosa* = 500 bow-lengths.[5]

26. Of these names none above *angula* have as yet been found in actual use as measures, and the same remark applies to *kukku, yaṭṭhi,* and *kosa.* Vidatthi (the span) has been found in the Pátimokkha, the rest occur only in the literature of the fifth century after Christ. The líksha occurs as a measure of weight in Mr. Thomas's table, p. 13, and most of the above names as measures of length in his table at p. 31, where Sanskrit calculations, greatly differing from the above Páli ones, will be found. Taking the vidatthi[6] or span at 8½ to 9 inches, and the ratana[7] or cubit, (which should be measured from the elbow to the end of the *little* finger only, see § 30) at from 17 to 18 inches, the yojana, according to Moggallána's scale, would be equal to between 12 and 12½ miles, and this is the length given by Childers; but I think it is certain that no such scale as Moggallána here gives was ever practically used in Ceylon. The finger joint, span, and cubit, may have been used for short lengths; the usabha for longer ones; the gávuta and yojana for paths or roads; but I doubt whether any attempt was made in practice to bring these different measures into one scheme.

27. In trying to draw up such schemes, Moggallána has been compelled to make arbitrary assumptions, and to put in imaginary measures, to which he has given the names he found in the Sanskrit lexicographers, without troubling himself much whether he changed their relative values or not. As regards the larger measures of length, I have noted the following few passages; it is only from a comparison of lists of such passages, making them as complete and accurate as possible, and allowing due weight to the various ages and countries of the authors, that a trustworthy estimate can be formed of the sense in which these measures were really used.

[1] See Dhammapada (ed. Fausböll), pp. 319–21; Pátimokkha (ed. Minayeff), pp. 76, 78, 81, 16; Mahávamsa (ed. Turnour), p. 169.

[2] This is the usual word. See *e.g.* Dhp., p. 168, Mahávamsa, pp. 141 and 257, line 7, and Ját. pp. 34–44.

[3] This is inserted from verse 197.

[4] Usabha is used in the Mahávansa, pp. 133, 153, and in the commentary quoted by Alwis, Intr. p. 79. The river Anomá, at the place where Gautama cut off his hair, is said at Játaka, p. 64, line 22, to be 8 usabhas, and in the Manual of Buddhism, p. 161, to be 800 cubits, broad. Compare Big. p. 212.

[5] Compare Mr. Thomas's Essay, p. 32, and the Appendix to Cunningham's Ancient Geography of India, vol. i.

[6] The 'Buddha's span' (Pátimokkha, iv. 6; vii. 87–92) was longer.

[7] Sanskrit *aratni.* Only found in this sense in a commentary quoted by Alwis, Introduction to Kaccáyana's Pali Grammar, p. 76, line 21, and at Jataka, p. 7.

TABULATED STATEMENT OF PASSAGES ON THE LENGTH OF THE YOJANA.

	Names of Places.		Distance according to Buddhist text.	Direct distance on modern maps in miles.	No. of miles in a yojana.[1]	Authorities.
1.	Benares	to Uruvela	18 yojanas.	128	8	Játaka, p. 68, l. 5, p. 81, l. 24; Big. pp. 51, 74; Hardy, Man. B., p. 184.[2]
2.	do.	,, Takshila	120 do.	850	7½	Játaka, 395; comp. Dhp. 384.
3.	Kapilavastu	,, The River Anomá	6 do.	40–45	?8	Gya Tchér Rol Pa, p. 214.
4.	do.	,, do.	30 do.	do.	?	Játaka, p. 64, line 16; Big., p. 41; Hardy, M. B., p. 161.
5.	The River Anomá	,, Rájagriha	30 do.	?	?	Játaka, p. 66, line 1; Big., p. 44; Hardy, M. B., p. 162.
6.	Nálanda	,, do.	1 do.	8	8	Turnour, J.B.A.S. vii. 998.
7.	Kapilavastu	,, do.	60 do.	210	?4	Játaka, p. 87, line 16; Big., p. 116; Hardy, M. B., p. 199.
8.	Kusinagara	,, do.	25 do.	150	7	Bigandet, p. 212.
9.	Ṣrávasti	,, do.	45 do.	275	7	Játaka, p. 92, line 20; Big., p. 126; Hardy, M. B., p. 218.[3]
10.	The Ganges	,, do.	5 do.	35	8	Hardy, M. B., p. 237.
11.	do.	,, Vaiṣáli	3 do.	24	8½	,, ,,
12.	Ṣrávasti	,, do.	54 do.	225	6	,, p. 282.
13.	Kapilavastu	,, do.	49–51 do.	160	?4	,, p. 310; 341.
14.	Ṣrávasti	,, Álavaka	30 do.	?	?	,, p. 261.
15.	Áloka	,, do.	3 do.	do.	?	,, p. 262.
16.	Patna	,, Rakshita	100 do.	?	?	Ib. p. 515, from Milinda Paṇha.
17.	do.	,, The Bo-Tree	7 do.	60	8½	Mahávansa, p. 111.
18.	Ságala	,, Kashmír	12 do.	100–180	?	Milinda Paṇha, Alwis, Intro. p. xliii., Hardy, M B., p. 516.
19.	do.	,, Alexandria	200 do.	88 *or* 260 *or* 360	?	Milinda Paṇha, do.
20.	Sankassa	,, Ṣrávasti	30 do.	?	?	Hardy, M.B. p. 300; Bigandet, p. 213.
21.	do.	,, Madhurá	4 do.	?	?	Kaccáyana (Senart, p. 129).[4]
22.	Rájagriha	,, Laṭṭhivana	3 gávutas.	?	?	Hardy, M.B. 191. Big. 142. Ját. 84, 6.
23.	The Bo-Tree	,, Yosisa	do.	?	?	Bigandet, p. 74.
24.	Kusinagara	,, Pává	do.	?	?	Big., p. 174; Hardy, M. B., p. 344.
25.	Anurádhapura	,, {The Maháwæli ganga, at the Kaccaka ferry}	9 yojanas.	70	9	Mahávansa, p. 139.
26.	do.	,, do. at Tambapiṭṭhi	7 do.	50	8	,, p. 166.
27.	do.	,, Ácárawiṭṭhi-gáma	3 do.	?	?	,, p. 166.
28.	do.	,, Sumana-vápi	4 do.	do.	?	,, p. 166.
29.	do.	,, The Ridi Wihára	8 do.	54	7¾	,, p. 167.
30.	do.	,, Adam's Peak	15 do.	100	7½	Beal's Fa Hian, p. 150.

28. Disregarding the cases in which Kapilavastu is mentioned—concerning the site of which place there is still some doubt—the average of the list is rather less than eight miles to the yojana. What is of more importance, a careful consideration of those data which are most certain leads to a similar result. Among these the two last are the most important. Fa Hian visited Anurádhapura

[1] In each case about one-sixth has been added to allow for the difference between the direct distance and the distance by roads or paths.

[2] Spence Hardy here and usually has translated the distances into miles, reckoning the yojana at 16 miles; see p. 160, where 480 miles in one sentence = 30 yojanas in the next; and see also p. 199. Beal, pp. 245, 246, gives the names of places on the way between these two towns, but compare Bigandet, *loc. cit.*

[3] The places on the route are given by Hardy, M. B., p. 335.

[4] This distance is quite inconsistent with Cunningham's identification of Sankassa, Ancient Geog. p. 369, with which, however, No. 20 agrees.

about 413 A.D., when Mahánáma, the author of the Mahávansa, must have been still a lad. As he did not himself visit Adam's Peak, his statement that it was fifteen yojanas from Anurádhapura must have been derived from the monks there, and—there being no doubt as to the actual distance—is very good evidence of the value they attached to the word. Still more trustworthy is the conclusion to be drawn from No. 29. The Ambalaṭṭhi-kola Lena mentioned by Mahánáma is well known to be the site of the still-celebrated Ridi Wihára in the Kurunægala district,[1] and its distance from Anurádhapura must have been well known to the monks at the latter place; the path from one to the other lay through the then most populous part of Ceylon, and is perfectly easy. In No. 19 we have to choose between four different Alexandrias, not one of which at all agrees with the distance given:[2] and as regards No. 18, on which Childers lays so much stress, though General Cunningham has fixed the site of Ságala without doubt, "Kashmír" seems to me to be a very vague term. Nothing is known of the date of the author of Milinda Paṇha, in which the statement is found, or of the sources of his information; and the boundary of Kashmír was constantly extending and contracting in the direction of Ságala. It is true that the seat of government was usually fixed at about the same place, namely, at and near Ṣrí Nagara; but as this is 180-190 miles from Ságala, the yojana would then equal about 17½ miles, which is so highly unlikely to have been intended, that we may safely reject the interpretation. In No. 1 the distance given in the books is not from Benares itself, but from the Migadaya garden near it, where Gautama preached his first sermon, and which probably lay, according to Cunningham, about half a yojana to the north of the town.

29. The conclusion to which I come is that we have no data as yet for determining the sense in which the word yojana is used in the Three Piṭakas; that in the fifth-century Páli literature it means between seven and eight miles,[3] and that the traditions preserved by Ceylon authors of that date as to distances in North India in the time of Gautama agree pretty well, except in the cases of Kapilavastu and Sankassa, with the sites fixed by General Cunningham.

30. Moggallána[4] further gives *tála*, *gokaṇṇa* and *padesa* as names of a short span; but in the only passage given by Childers where tála (which means palmyra-tree) is used to express length, it means "the height of a palm-tree." The other words have not been found in the texts. I presume Moggallána means the three words to express the length when the hand is extended from the end of the thumb to the ends of the three centre figures respectively, *vidatthi* being the name for the ordinary span to the end of the fourth or little finger. Finally, Moggallána gives[5] *Vyáma* as the length a man can stretch with both arms, that is, a fathom; and *Porisa* (literally manliness) as the length a man can reach up to when his arms are held over his head. The latter does not seem to have been in actual use; on the other hand *yuga*, a yoke, is used to

[1] See Turnour in the Index s.v., and compare Mahávansa, p. 167, with da Zoysa's account of Ridi Wihára in his Report on Temple Libraries, 1875.

[2] For Alexandria Opiane see Cunningham's Ancient Geography of India, vol. i. p. 24, and for the three others do. Map V. p. 104.

[3] As when Professor Childers, in his Dictionary, s.v., looks upon the yojana "as about equivalent to twelve miles," he is following Moggallána, though he especially instances No. 16, so also when the Burmese make it = 13½ miles (teste Rogers, Bud. Par. p. 42), this probably rests on some similar calculation.

[4] Verse 267. They are also given in the Amara Kosha, 2, 6, 2, 34.

[5] Verse 269; and see Childers, s.v.

express length, and Spence Hardy renders it the distance of a plough or nine spans[1] (*i.e.* 6-7 feet); and *hatthapása* occurs (Pátimokkha, Dickson, p. 11; Kankhá Vitaraní, Minayeff, p. 98) in the sense of 2½ cubits.

31. At the end of his scheme of measures of length, Moggallána states that a *karisa* is equal to four ammaṇas (a superficial measure). *Karísa* seems to have been the measure of extent really in use in Ceylon in the fifth century; it is used quite independently of ammaṇa (which does not occur as a measure of extent till much later). Eight *karisas* are mentioned in the Mahávansa, p. 221, l. 40, in the commentaries to the Dhammapada (p. 135), and to the Játaka (p. 94, l. 24); sixteen *karisas* in the Mahávansa (p. 166), and in the Játaka commentary (p. 94, l. 22); and again one hundred *karisas* in the Mahávansa, p. 61. None of these passages give any clue to its size; but if the tradition preserved by Moggallána be correct, it would be equal to about four acres. Like all other Ceylon measures of extent, it is derived, not from any measure of length, but from a measure of capacity, the Tamil karísu, explained by Winslow to be a dry measure equal to four hundred marakkáls, or according to some equal to two hundred paras. It was not till after the arrival of the Europeans that the Sinhalese had any exact measure of extent: they *always measured land by the quantity of seed which could be sown in it;* and the peasantry do so still in practice, although in some of the more advanced districts they occasionally use English measures in their legal documents. One result of their mode of measurement is that each measure varies according to the nature of the ground, and the kind of seed used. Thus a pæla[2] of land on very dry soil, where rice will not grow, or on a hill-side, where the seed has to be sown very sparsely, is larger than a pæla of muddy or low land, where the ordinary rice will grow very thickly. To add to the confusion, the dry measures of capacity differ in different districts, not only different names being generally used, but the same name in different senses.[3]

32. This was doubtless the case also in the twelfth century, when Moggallána drew up the following table of

MEASURES OF CAPACITY.

4	Pasata (handfuls)[4] or Kuḍuba*	= 1	Pattha or Náḷi.									
16	do.	= 4	do.	= 1	Aḷhaka or Tumba.*							
64	do.	= 16	do.	= 4	do.	= 1	Doṇa.					
256	do.	= 64	do.	= 16	do.	= 4	do.	= 1	Máṇiká.*			
1024	do.	= 256	do.	= 64	do.	= 16	do.	= 4	do.	= 1	Khárí.*	
20480	do.	= 5120	do.	= 1280	do.	= 320	do.	= 80	do.	= 20	do.	= 1 Váha (horse load), Sakaṭa (cart load).

Also 11 Doṇa = 1 Ammana, and 10 Ammaṇa = 1 Kumbha.*

33. Of these none of those marked * are used in the sense of a measure in the published texts, unless the statement in Kaccáyana (Senart, p. 155) that a *doṇa* is less than a khárí can be

[1] Manual Buddh. p. 371; comp. Dickson, Pátimokkha, p. 59.

[2] The æ to be pronounced like French è in *mère.*

[3] Clough, in his Dictionary, says 5 kurunis or yálas = 1 parrah; 12 kurunis = 1 pæla; and 8 parrahs or 160 measures = 1 amuna. I have usually found that 40 láhas were = 1 pæla, and 4 pælas = 1 amuna (Páli ammana), which was in rice-fields equal to about two acres. Compare on this mode of measuring extent, Thomas, Ancient Indian Weights, p. 31, note; and Colebrooke, Miscellaneous Essays, vol. ii. p. 245.

[4] Pasata is really the cavity formed by bending the palm of one hand; that formed by joining the two hands is called karapuṭa, or añjali. See Abh. 286 and Mah. 37.

considered as an example of the use of khárí; but curiously enough *khárí* occurs at Játaka, p. 9, lines 15, 24 as a measure of weight. Moggallána follows the current Sanskrit tables except in the data regarding the váha, ammaṇa, and kumbha; and in the omission of the measures less than the pasata, by which the Sanskrit tables establish an artificial connexion between this table and the tables of weight.[1] The ammaṇa (Sinhalese amuṇa, Tamil ambana) now varies in different parts of Ceylon from five to seven bushels and a half. In the Mahávansa, pp. 174, 157, an ammaṇa of sand is mentioned; at Ját. 33 an ammaṇa of kahápaṇas; and at Játaka, p. 62, line 15, we are told of a mattrass made of an ammaṇa of jasmine and other flowers.

34. In the commentary on the Pátimokkha[2] occurs the following interesting passage: 'There are three kinds of begging bowls—the high bowl, the middle bowl, and the low bowl. The high bowl takes half an *áḷhaka* of boiled rice (or the fourth of that quantity of uncooked rice) and a suitable supply of curry: the middle bowl takes a *náḷiká*[3] of boiled rice (or the fourth of that quantity of uncooked rice) and a suitable supply of curry: the low bowl takes a *pattha* of boiled rice (or the fourth of that quantity of uncooked rice) and a suitable supply of curry. From some places the high bowl cannot be procured, from others the low bowl. In this passage 'three kinds of bowls' means three sizes of bowls; 'takes half an áḷhaka of boiled rice' means takes the boiled food made from two náḷis of dry rice of the Magadha náḷi. In the Andha Commentary[4] a Magadha náḷi is said to be 13½ handfuls (*pasatas*). The náḷi in use in the island of Ceylon is larger than the Tamil one. The Magadha náḷi is the right measure. It is said in the Great Commentary that one Sinhalese náḷi is equal to 1½ of this Magadha náḷi.' It is clear from the above passage that Moggallána's scheme, in which the pattha is made the same as the náḷi, will not apply to the fifth-century books. The náḷi was a liquid as well as a dry measure, for a náḷi of oil is mentioned at Mahávansa, p. 177, l. 6, and a náḷi of honey at Mahávansa, p. 197, l. 1. At Játaka, p. 98, l. 5, Gaütama tells a householder to listen, giving ear attentively, as if he were filling a golden náḷi with lion's marrow! The original meaning of the word is *pipe* or *reed*, then the joint of a bambú, and hence the measure, either dry or liquid, which such a joint would contain; or, as a measure of extent, the space over which the seed contained in such a measure could be sown.[5] As the size of different bambus differed, we can understand the origin of the difference in the size of the measures. In Sanskrit, though neither náḍi nor náḷi have acquired the meaning of a measure of capacity, náḍi is given in the Koṣas as a measure of time.[6] The corresponding measure of capacity in Sanskrit is prastha, to which in the Peṭersburg Dictionary many different values are assigned, *inter alia* that of four Kudavas; and it is curious to notice that Colebrooke (Essays, vol. ii. p. 535) mentions a 'Magadha prastha,' which the Tibetans also use (Táranátha, p. 35). The Sinhalese word is næḷiya,[7] which Clough explains as 'three pints, wine measure:' the Tamil is

[1] See Thomas, *loc. cit.* p. 26, and Colebrooke, Amara Kosha, p. 242, where 20 Droṇas = 1 Kumbha; and 10 Kumbha (*i.e.* 200 and not 320 Doṇa) = 1 Váha. Compare Colebrooke's Essays, vol. ii. pp. 533-538.

[2] Minayeff, p. 81 on 10, 19.

[3] This of course is the same as náḷi. See Játaka, pp. 124-126.

[4] See Minayeff's Pátimokkha, p. viii. note 11, and Wijesinha's paper on the origin of the Buddhist Commentaries, in the Journal of the Royal Asiatic Society for 1871, p. 10 (of the separate edition).

[5] Comp. Wilson, Glossary, s.v., and Traill's Report on Kumāon, As. Res. xiv.

[6] At Mahávansa, p. 227, last line, kuntanáḷi seems to mean the handle, or perhaps sheath, of a spear or dagger.

[7] The æ pronounced like *a* in *hat*.

náḷi, which Winslow explains as the eighth part of a kurundi or marakkál. Finally, in the inscription referred to above (§ 20), *yála, kiriya,* and *paya* are used as measures of extent; the kiriya being four ammaṇas: and *nœḷiya, aḍamaná,* and *pata* are used as measures of capacity; the pata being the same as pasata, a handful, and stated by Clough to be the eighth of a seer, that is, the 256th part of a bushel, while the aḍamaná is probably another name for the náḷi.

PART III.

Sketch of the History of Ceylon under those Kings whose Coins are extant.[1]

35. About five centuries before Christ the island of Ceylon was colonized by Aryan settlers from Orissa. On their arrival they found the country inhabited by a people whom in their histories they called Yakshas or devils, and who were probably of Draviḍian race, although their nationality has not yet been, and probably never will be, ascertained with certainty.[2] The island was converted to Buddhism in the middle of the third century B.C. by Mahendra, the son of Aṣóka the Great; but was very soon afterwards invaded by the Tamils, who held the whole of the Northern plains for more than half a century. From that time down to the fourteenth century the history of Ceylon is the history of the struggles of the Aryan islanders to hold their own against the ever-increasing numbers of the Draviḍian hordes. Twelve times the Tamils became masters of the plains, and twelve times the Sinhalese issued forth again from their mountain strongholds and drove their enemies back across the sea. But each victory left the victors weaker than before. They felt they were fighting against overwhelming odds, and gradually withdrew the seat of government further and further south, until the long struggle was terminated at last by the devastation of the country; and the rich plains from the peninsula of Jaffna in the extreme North to the Northerly spurs of the Central hills relapsed into their present state of almost deserted jungle.

36. In the last years of the tenth century the Cholians had been obliged to quit the island; but in the year 1050 they again invaded Ceylon, and though the King had fled to the hills in the South, they captured him and his Queen, and carried them prisoners to the peninsula. As soon as they turned their backs, the mountaineers, as usual, reasserted their independence; and while the plains were governed by the Cholian viceroy, the hills were ruled by a son of the captured King named Káṣyapa. The King died in captivity, but his son immediately proclaimed himself Rája of Ceylon, and was making great preparations to expel the Cholians, when he was taken ill and died. Always dependent on a visible head, the Sinhalese were at once thrown into disorder. The young son of Káṣyapa was proclaimed King, and his advisers sent for help to Siam—not altogether without

[1] The authorities are: Turnour's Epitome of the History of Ceylon, and his Mahávansa, pp. lxiv-lxvii and lxxxvi-lxxxix; Lassen's Indische Alterthumskunde, vol. iv. pp. 309-336, for which Lassen has used a MS of the Mahávansa; and my articles, 'On the Invasion of South India by Parákrama the Great,' in the Journ. Bengal As. Soc., vol. xli. part 1, 1872; 'On the Audience Hall Inscription' in the Indian Antiquary for Sept., 1873, and 'On Sinhalese Inscriptions' in the Journ. Royal As. Soc. for 1874 and 1875. For the period subsequent to Parákrama's death I have also consulted the MS. of the Mahávansa in the India Office.

[2] It has been usual to consider the Wæddas, a tribe of savages still existing in the South-west jungles of Ceylon, as the descendants of these aborigines. If this be so, they were possibly the descendants of former Aryan colonists, but the language of the Wæddas has not yet been thoroughly investigated. Mr. B. F. Hartshorne, late of the Ceylon Civil Service, has stated all that is known of this curious tribe in an interesting article in the *Fortnightly Review* of January last.

success; but the central power was too weak to gain hearty allegiance; the clans retired to their valleys; and for a time the national cause seemed to be forgotten, whilst the members of the royal family were engaged in schemes against each other. At last the rivalry broke out in open revolt, and two chiefs, near relations of the young King WIJAYA-BÁHU, proclaimed war against him. The danger of the crisis showed that Wijaya-báhu had inherited his father's martial vigour. He himself took the field, and completely defeated the insurgents; and at the first news of the victory, the clans flocked to his standard. Then ensued a protracted and desultory warfare, which did not end till the Cholians were completely driven out of the island. The King established his Court at Pulastipura, and spent the last ten years of his long reign in endeavours to restore the irrigation works on which depended the prosperity of the country, and which had fallen into decay under the rule of the Malabars.

37. But the unfortunate country was not to taste the blessings of peace. Immediately on the death of the King, the members of the royal family, who thought only of their own interests, began to quarrel for the possession of the throne, and for twenty-two years the island was desolated by a civil war of the most ruthless and determined kind. At length PARÁKRAMA BÁHU (1153), a nephew of the late King, after a long struggle with his uncles, and a short but bitter and furious war against his own father, was able to crown himself King of all Ceylon, and enjoy the sweet sense of undisputed power. He was not long in showing that that power would be used to a degree to which it had never been used before. He strongly fortified his capital Pulastipura, the modern Topáwa, built a splendid palace seven stories high for himself, and two others five stories high for priests and devotees. Then he laid out a park near his palace, and built in it a hall for the coronation of kings, and near it a brick temple, which he called the Jetawanáráma.[1] At the other end of the town he constructed also a splendid stone temple for the worship of the Buddha—a building which, carved out of the solid rock, is, even in its ruins, a lasting memorial of the skill and taste of the workmen he employed. In a few years he had succeeded, partly by taxation, partly by compulsory labour, in making Pulastipura one of the strongest and most beautiful cities in India; and he succeeded also in rousing into rebellion a nation always distinguished for its wondrous patience under the oppression of its kings.[2] The insurrection was put down after a protracted struggle, causing great destruction of life and property, and a severe example was made among the insurgents, the leaders being impaled, beheaded and otherwise punished. Once more unrivalled at home, this able and ambitious despot now turned his victorious arms against the Kings of Kámboja and Rámánya,[3] undeterred by the enormous risk and difficulty of sending a fleet of transports 1500 miles from home to the further side of the open Bay of Bengal. It may well be doubted whether any other monarch in Europe or Asia would at that time have conceived so daring an idea, or, if he had, could have carried it to a successful issue. The Crusaders carried their arms about as far;

[1] By the kind permission of Mr. Fergusson I have been allowed to place at the beginning of this monograph the woodcut of this temple, which originally appeared in Sir E. Tennent's Ceylon. Since the drawing from which it was taken was made, the entrance was excavated for Government under my superintendence, and was found to be richly carved in bas-relief.

[2] It seems probable, from the headings of the chapters of the Mahávansa relating to this period, that some of the disappointed members of the royal family took advantage of the general discontent to incite the people to revolt.

[3] *i.e.* Burma; and more especially its coast provinces referred to in Aṣoka's edicts as *Suvaṇṇa-bhúmi*. Comp. Bigandet, p. 389.

but they either marched through countries for the most part friendly, or sailed along the Mediterranean, whose numerous islands could afford them food and shelter: and though they accomplished much which they did not intend, they failed in the object they proposed. About 1175 A.D. the Sinhalese fleet arrived safely at its destination, and completely conquered Kákadvípa and Rámánya, taking the Kings of those countries, with their ministers, prisoners. The latter was restored to his throne on the monks interceding for him and on his making full submission; but the King of Kákadvípa died in captivity in Ceylon.

38. Soon afterwards the Páṇḍian King Parákrama, of the city of Madura, appealed to his Sinhalese namesake for help against his suzerain Kulasekhara, who was preparing to attack him. The flattering request was received with favour, and a Sinhalese army was sent to invade and lay waste the territories of Kulasekhara, that King being taken prisoner, and his son Vírapáṇḍu raised to the throne as a vassal of Parákrama Báhu. About 1180 the troops advanced also against Chola, and after an obstinate war took and destroyed the strongly fortified capital Amarávatí, and then returned to Ceylon rich with booty and tribute. Meanwhile the King at home had been still further adding to the religious and royal buildings at his capital, and had undertaken some of the largest and most difficult engineering works which the mind of man had then conceived. He constructed inland lakes ten, twenty, even forty miles round (one of them called 'the Sea of Parákrama'), fed from the principal rivers of Ceylon by broad and deep canals, which also united these lakes to one another and to the principal towns, whilst smaller canals conducted their waters to extensive and fertile tracts of arable land. It may perhaps be doubtful whether all of these works were worth the immense labour which they must have cost; but as the labour was probably compulsory, whilst a tax in kind of one-tenth of the produce was certainly levied on all the irrigated land, the schemes no doubt benefited the royal exchequer, while they threw additional glory on the royal name. Parákrama died in 1186, after a reign of thirty-three years—'the most martial, enterprising and glorious,' says Turnour, 'in Sinhalese history'; he had earned for himself undying fame, and had so exhausted and impoverished the country that it was long before it began to recover from the effects of his daring ambition.

39. The following table will show the relationship of Parákrama to his different rivals in Ceylon.

MAHENDRA IV. (1023 A.D.)

Káṣyapa Wikrama-báhu

WIJAYA-BÁHU I. (1071) Wíra-báhu Jaya-báhu I. (1126) Mittá = a Páṇḍyan prince.

Wikrama-báhu Subhadrá Ratnávalí = Manábarana Kirti Ṣrí Meghawarṇa Ṣrí Wallabha

Lilávatí = PARÁKRAMA I. = Rupáwalí

40. Parákrama was succeeded by his nephew WIJAYA BÁHU (1186), whose character seems to have been a curious mixture. He is celebrated in the priestly chronicles as a most religious prince,

who himself wrote letters in the sacred language to exhort the King of Rámánya to aid him in extending the faith, and who took great pains to administer impartial justice, and relieved the people from the oppressions under which they had been suffering under his predecessor. But it was an intrigue with a farmer's daughter named Dípaní which led to his being murdered, after a reign of only one year, by a Kálingan named Mahinda.

41. The throne was then seized by the crown prince (uparaja) NIṢṢANKA MALLA (1187), a relation of Parákrama's Queen Lílávatí, and a son of Rája Jayagopa of Kalinga. The Mahávansa, after describing at great length in eighteen chapters the striking acts of Parákrama, unfortunately dismisses the next sixteen kings in one short chapter, and the deficiency is only partly made up by the interesting inscriptions referred to in the note at the commencement of this historical sketch. It appears from these inscriptions that Niṣṣanka Malla was a quiet and patriotic, if not very vigorous or wise prince, who devoted the nine short years of his reign to internal reforms. He visited all parts of the island, and boasted that 'such was the security which he established, that even a woman might pass through the land with a precious gem and not be asked, "What is it?"'[1] The means by which he accomplished this may not have been so foolish as at first sight it appears. 'He put down robbery,' says the Ruwanwæli Inscription, 'by relieving—through gifts of cattle and fields and gold and silver and money[2] and pearls and jewelry and clothes, as each one desired—the anxiety of the people, who, impoverished and oppressed by the very severe taxations of Parákrama Báhu the First (which exceeded those customary by former kings), lived by robbery: for, thought he, they wish to steal only because they desire to live.' He further claims to have reduced taxation, remitting entirely one tax—that on hill paddy—which was felt as a particular hardship, and at the same time to have greatly improved internal communication, repairing the roads and putting up rest-houses along them for the use of travellers. 'Removing far away the fear of poverty and the fear of thieves and the fear of oppression, he made every one in the island of Lanká happy.' But he lavished enormous sums on the priests. He is said, in one Inscription, to have spent seven laks on the Cave Temple at Dambulla, and forty laks on the Ruwanwæli Dágaba at Anurádhapura;[3] and though these amounts are certainly exaggerated (another of his own inscriptions giving them as one and seven laks), he is known to have built the huge Rankot Dágaba at Pulastipura, and the exquisite stone temple of the Tooth at the same place, certainly the most beautiful, though one of the smallest ancient temples in Ceylon.

42. His son Wírabáhu was killed on the day of his accession, and his brother Wikrama Báhu, who succeeded, suffered the same fate three months afterwards, at the hands of his son or nephew CODAGANGA (1196), who, after a short reign of nine months, was dethroned and blinded by the minister Kirti. The minister then married LÍLÁWATÍ, the widow of Parákrama, and ruled the

[1] Hallam in his 'Middle Ages,' vol. ii. p. 312, quotes from the Saxon Chronicler that in the time of William the Conqueror 'a girl laden with gold might have passed safely through the kingdom.' And Tennyson makes Harold say to the Earl of Porthieu:

> 'In mine earldom
> A man may hang gold bracelets on a bush,
> And leave them for a year, and coming back
> Find them again.'

[2] *masu ran*, i.e. gold másakas.

[3] Forbes's Ceylon, vol. ii. p. 347.

country in her name for the next three years. They were in their turn overthrown by another minister Aṇikanga, who first placed SÁHASA MALLA, another son (but by a different queen) of Rája Jayagopa, of Kalinga, on the throne,[1] but deposed and banished him after two years, and then reigned for six years in the name of KALYÁNAWATÍ, the widow of Niṣṣanka Malla. Her son (?) DHARMÁSOKA DEVA, a babe of three months old, was the next puppet king, but after governing in his name for a year, Aṇikanga, relying on the help of Cholian mercenaries, put him to death, and openly declared himself King. But he had gone too far. Another revolution or palace intrigue immediately took place: after a few days he was captured and killed, and Líláwatí was restored to the throne. But before she had enjoyed her recovered dignity for a year, another insurrection broke out, which ended, twenty-eight months after her restoration, by a Páṇḍian prince named PARÁKRAMA (1211) attaining supreme power. He also was not long left in peace. A new invasion—this time from Kalinga[2]—took place, and a barbarian prince named MÁGHA (1214) overran the island, pillaging and destroying the temples and oppressing the people.

43. After tyrannizing over the unhappy country for twenty-one years, this despot was attacked by a young chief named Wijaya-báhu, who rallied round his standard the brave mountaineers —always the last to be subdued, and the first to revolt.[3] In a desperate struggle, which lasted three years,[4] they regained from their oppressors first the mountain districts, then the plains of Ruhuna in the South, and at last the capital Pulastipura and the plains of the North.[5] But the latter city had been completely ruined, and when the patriot chief was crowned King of all Ceylon, under the title of WIJAYA BÁHU III., in 1235, he removed the seat of government to Dambadenia, at the foot of the Kandian hills in the district now called Kurunaègala.

44. In his long reign of twenty-four years this patriotic ruler so strengthened the country that when the hereditary foes of Ceylon again invaded the island, in the time of his son PAṆḌITA PARÁKRAMA (1259), they met with a signal defeat. Both these monarchs were great patrons of literature; and the latter especially, who was himself a voluminous writer, took great pains to restore the sacred books, many of which had been destroyed in the time of Mágha, and caused the chronicles of the island to be completed down to his reign. His son WIJAYA BÁHU IV. returned to the ill-omened city of Pulastipura, and there, after he had reigned only two years, was murdered by his prime minister, Mitra Sena. But the latter did not live to reap the fruits of his treason. He was himself assassinated shortly after, and BHUWANAIKA BÁHU, the last of the kings whose coins are extant, succeeded to the vacant throne in 1296.

[1] The date of this event (1743 Anno Buddhæ = 1200 A.D.) is fixed by an inscription I have published in the Journal of the R.A.S. 1875, in an article entitled 'Two Sinhalese Inscriptions.' This is the oldest inscription but one as yet known in which Buddha-warsha, the era of Buddha, is mentioned; comp. § 84 below.

[2] Also called Keraḷa in the 80th chapter of the Mahávansa, verses 61, 76, of the India Office MS.

[3] That this Wijaya-báhu was not related to any of the preceding kings, is proved by the fact that be based his claim to the throne on his descent from Sanga Bo, a popular Sinhalese hero and Buddhist martyr, who reigned from A.D. 238–240. So Dhátusena, who expelled the Páṇḍian usurpers in the fifth century, claimed descent from Yaṭṭhála Tissa, who reigned in the first. Mah. pp. 218, 254.

[4] Lassen, *l.c.*, p. 337, note, thinks this should be seven years.

[5] When excavating at Pulastipura, I found at the ruined gate of the palace a fallen slab covered with an inscription of Niṣṣanka Malla. Under it was an old spear-head, which must have been used, at the latest, at this last siege of the ill-fated town, whose glory lasted so short a time.

45. List of the Kings of Ceylon from 1153–1296 a.d.

1.	Parákrama Báhu*	1153	
2.	Wijaya Báhu II.*	1186	Nephew of last.
3.	Nissanka Malla*	1187	A prince of Kalinga.
4.	Wikrama Báhu II.	1196	Brother of Nissanka Malla.
5.	Codaganga*	1196	Nephew of Nissanka Malla.
6.	Líláwatí* (queen)	1197	Widow of Parákrama Báhu.
7.	Sáhasa Malla*	1200	Brother (?) of Nissanka Malla.
8.	Kalyánawati (queen)	1202	Widow of Nissanka Malla.
9.	Dharmásoka*	1208	
10.	Líláwatí (restored)	1209	
11.	Pándi Parákrama Báhu	1211	Malabar usurper.
12.	Mágha	1214	A Kálingan prince.
13.	Dambadeniya Wijaya Báhu	1235	Founder of a new dynasty.
14.	Dambadeniya Parákrama	1259	Son of the last king.
15.	Bosat Wijaya Báhu	1294	Son of the last king.
16.	Bhunaweka Báhu*	1296	Brother of the last king.

* Coins are extant of those monarchs marked with a star.

PART IV. Description of the Coins.

Coins of Parákrama Báhu, 1153–1186 a.d.

46. *The Lankeswara gold coin*, Figs. 1, 2, 3, 4.

On the obverse a standing figure of the king; turning towards the right; in his left hand a lotus-flower, of which Fig. 3 gives a front view, the others a side view; in his right hand apparently a weapon of some kind,[1] figured most clearly in Fig. 4. To the left of this is another symbol, appearing most clearly in Fig. 4, the meaning of which I do not understand (? a sceptre). The figure stands on the stalk of a lotus terminating in a flower to its left; between this flower and the left hand are five dots surrounded by small circles, which again I take to be lotus-flowers. Fig. 3 has only four of these. The dhoti or cloth wrapped round the loins falls in folds on each side of and between the legs.[2] On the head of the figure is a conical cap.

On the reverse the same figure seated. In the left hand a lotus [there is nothing in the

[1] Prinsep, ed. Thomas, vol. i. p. 421, calls it 'an instrument of warfare.' Mr. Vaux, Numismatic Chronicle, vol. i. xvi. p. 124, calls it trisula, that is, trident. This it can scarcely be, as it has four points, not three, and is quite different from the trisula in Fig. 19. It may possibly be a flower, and is, in any case, an ancient symbol.

[2] Prinsep says that some, mistaking this for a tail, have supposed the figure to be Hanumán. The only writer I have been able to find advocating this opinion is Simon Casie Chitty, in a paper in the Journal of the Ceylon Asiatic Society for 1845, p. 82. It may be as well to point out that Hanumán, 'the mighty-jawed,' the mythical monkey who appears in the Rámáyana as the faithful ally of Ráma in his fabled invasion of Ceylon, is almost unknown in Sinhalese literature, and was never worshipped in the island. The true origin of the figure is explained below, § 65, and there can be no reason to believe that the Sinhalese meant to represent a mythological monster, known only as an enemy to Ceylon.

right—the extension with five projections is meant for the hand with the five fingers].[1] The left leg rests on a kind of grating. On the left side of the figure, to the right of the coin, the legend श्री लंकेश्वर *Ṣri Lankeṣwara.*[2] In Fig. 3 the anuswára circle or dot is misplaced under the left arm of the figure. The complete form of the *e*, a small stroke to the upper right of the क, is very clear in Figs. 3 and 4, and is quite different from the *e* in the *deva* of Fig. 20. The *ṣ* over the व is also clear enough in Figs. 3 and 4. The र in all specimens is curiously like द, and unlike the र of rája, Fig. 21; and of Parákrama, Figs. 5, 6, 7, 11, 14, 15.

47. Prinsep[3] says of this coin, 'This name (Lankeṣwara) I presume to be the minister Lokaiṣwara of Mr. Turnour's table, who usurped the throne during the Cholian subjection in the eleventh century (A.D. 1060): but he is not included among the regular sovereigns, and the coin may therefore belong to another usurper of the same name who drove out Queen Lílávatí in A.D. 1215, and reigned for a year.' Mr. Vaux[4] adopts the former of these two suggestions; but the first part of the word, Lank-, is perfectly clear on several specimens of the coin (see Figs. 1 and 4). If Lokaiṣwara had struck a coin and had intended to put his name upon it, he would have done so; and the *o* represented in this alphabet by two substantial strokes, one on each side of the letter (see Fig. 22), could not have disappeared as the tiny anuswára dot has sometimes done.

48. The epithet Lankeṣwara, Lord of Ceylon, may apply to any king of that country, and the similarity of name is no reason for fixing it upon either of these Lokaiṣwaras. It should be noticed also that the former of the two was not a king at all, but a minister mentioned in the lists as the father of Wijaya Báhu I.; and the latter was a foreign usurper who never was in acknowledged possession of the kingdom, though he retained a precarious hold on the capital for a few months. Discarding therefore the idea that Lankeṣwara stands for Lokaiṣwara, we have to consider to which King of Ceylon this epithet belongs. It is never used in Ceylon literature before the time of Parákrama the Great. The Páli form Lankissara is then found applied to three kings; namely, to Mahasena, A.D. 275, and his son Kirti Ṣrí Megha-warṇa, A.D. 301;[5] and to Wijaya Báhu the First, A.D. 1071.[6] The Sinhalese form is only found applied to two kings; namely, to Parákrama Báhu himself in the account of his conquest of South India,[7] and to Niṣṣanka Malla, A.D. 1187, in his own inscriptions.[8] Coins were unknown in Ceylon in the time of the first two kings mentioned; it is not known that any were struck by the third. The epithet is used of him in such a way as to convey the impression rather that the word in the time of the writer (tempore Parákrama) had come to be used of all Kings of Ceylon, than that it was a distinctive appellation of Wijaya. There remain the two last; for the former speaks the fact that the word came into use in the literature of his reign; that he conquered South India, and thence introduced the art

[1] I think the object held by Fig. 3 is, like that in the others, meant for a lotus, but compare Fig. 12.

[2] Mr. Thomas altogether dissents from Prinsep's original reading of *Lankeṣvara*, and interprets the legible portion of the letters as लंकोवेह *Lankí Veha*, or in No. 4 लंकीविह *Lankí Viha*.

[3] Vol. i. p. 421 of Mr. Thomas's edition.

[4] Numismatic Chronicle, 1853, vol. xvi. p. 125.

[5] In the Dáṭhávansa, Canto v. verses 4, 60.

[6] Mahávansa, edit. Turnour, p. lxxxvi. Both this part of the Mahávansa and the Dáṭhávansa were written in the time of Parákrama.

[7] See my translation in the Journal of the B. A. S. for 1872, vol. xli. part 1, p. 199.

[8] In the Dambulla inscription, and in the Rankot Dágaba inscription, published by me in the Journal of the Royal Asiatic Society of 1874.

of coining into Ceylon;[1] and that he is the only King of Ceylon who struck several coins; for the latter that though in three of his inscriptions he is not called Lankeṣwara,[2] the epithet is given in two others as one of his distinctive titles. On the other hand, in those two inscriptions he is called *Kálinga* Lankeṣwara, and on his own coin he uses that title in full,[3] which is exactly what he would have done had he wished to distinguish himself from some previous Lankeṣwara.

On the whole, therefore, it seems to me certain—as certain, that is, as the identification of coins bearing such ambiguous legends ever can be—that this coin belongs to Parákrama the Great.

It only remains to add that the coin is rare. There are three examples in the Guthrie collection in Berlin, two in the British Museum, two in my own collection, and one in the collection of H. H. Bowman, Esq., of Baddegama, Ceylon. Those described by Prinsep and Mr. Vaux are in the British Museum.

No. 1 from my collection weighs 67 grains.[4] No. 2 is in the Guthrie collection. No. 3 is in the British Museum and weighs 68½ grains, though, as will be noticed, it is much less in diameter than the others. No. 4 is in the British Museum and weighs 65½ grains.

49. *The Lion coin of Parákrama*, Figs. 5, 6, 7. Copper.

On the obverse the standing figure of the rája. The face turned to right represented in the most extraordinary way by three strokes, with a curve for the back of the head. The transition form of this mode of expressing the face, which Prinsep calls 'altogether unique in the history of perverted art,' may be seen in Figs. 9, 11. In the left hand of the figure is the lotus, in the right the weapon referred to in § 46 and note 1. There is no lotus-stalk under the feet. The cap is formed by *two* strokes and a dot. The two dots under the arms are the upper part of the dhoti. To the right of the coin is a well-defined lion, sitting, with the mouth open, showing the teeth in the upper jaw.

On the reverse the seated figure of the rája, and to the right the legend श्री पराक्रमबाहु *Ṣri Parákrama Báhu.*

Fig. 5 is from the Guthrie collection. Fig. 6 from my own is worn, and weighs 55 grains. Fig. 7, also my own, weighs 61 grains. The British Museum has no specimen of this coin, of which less than a dozen examples have been found. My collection has seven of these, two in good condition, besides which I only know of Colonel Guthrie's, and of two others in private hands in Ceylon, one of which is now, I believe, in the possession of Mr. Bowman, and the other in Mr. Dickson's collection.

50. *The half massa of Parákrama Báhu.*

This small copper coin, Fig. 11, has on the obverse the standing figure of the rája, and on the reverse only the legend श्री पराक्रमबाहु *Sri Parákrama Báhu.* Prinsep, whose coins are now in the British Museum, says,[5] that 'several specimens of this were dug up in 1837 at Montollee (? Mátale) in Ceylon;' but the Museum has only four, of which the one figured in the Plate is the only one in good preservation, and no others are known to have reached Europe.

[1] See my article in the J. B. A. S. 1872, vol. xli. pt. 1, p. 197.

[2] Namely, the Ruwanwæli inscription published by me in the J. R. A. S. for 1875, and the two others in my article mentioned in the last note but one.

[3] See below § 66.

[4] A sovereign weighs nearly 170 grains.

[5] Loc. cit. p. 422, figure 4.

51. *The massa of Parákrama Báhu.* Figs. 14, 15.

On the obverse the standing figure as on the Lion coin. To the right beneath is a lotus, and above it five dots. On the reverse the sitting figure, and the legend श्री पराक्रमबाज़ *Sri Parákrama Báhu.* This is the coin which was imitated by the six succeeding rájas, and a good many specimens, perhaps 100 in all, have been found, but very few of them are in good condition, and scarcely any show the *r* at the foot of the *k.* Prinsep seems to have had only one.[1] The best specimen of fourteen in my collection weighs 62 grains.

52. The remainder of the coins, whose identification is certain, belong also to the series just mentioned; each of the following kings having only struck one coin. For the history of these kings the reader is referred to what has been said above; I quote here only the legends on the coins.

श्री विजयबाज़ *Ṣri Vijaya Báhu.* Fig. 17. Copper.

There were several kings so called; the coin belonging, I think, to the nephew and successor of Parákrama, the second of the name. It is almost certain that Parákrama the Great was the first King of Ceylon who issued coins, and the rarity of the specimens with this inscription agrees well with the shortness of Wijaya II.'s reign. The coin is rare; good examples very rare. The one in my collection, from which the figure is taken, weighs 62 grains.

53. श्री चोडगंगदेव *Ṣri Coḍaganga Deva.* Fig. 20. Copper.

This unique coin is in the possession of G. G. Plaice, Esq., late of the Public Works Department in Ceylon. I think there can be no doubt about the reading, though the anuswára is omitted, and the vowel marks of the *o* have pushed out the circle of the च. Turnour in his list has erroneously given the name of this king as Chondakanga, but the India Office MS. of the Mahávansa, ch. 80, clearly reads Coḍaganga.

54. श्री राजलीलावती *Ṣri Rája Lílávati.* Fig. 21.

This is not so rare as the Wijaya Báhu. The figure is taken from a specimen in my collection weighing 64 grains.

55. श्री मत्साहसमल्ल *Ṣri-mat Sáhasa Malla.* Fig. 23.

Some hundreds of these coins have been found. The curious shape of the square *s*, and the addition of the syllable *mat*, prevented its identification for some time, and Prinsep was the first to decipher it. The *t* is inserted in the upper left-hand corner of the square *s*, and is so small that in most of the specimens it is indistinguishable. The one in my collection from which the figure is taken weighs 63 grains. It is curious that no coins have as yet been discovered of Kalyánavatí, the queen who reigned for six years after the dethronement of Sáhasa Malla. It is true that more of his coins have been found than of any of the others, so that he may very possibly have issued more coins than were needed to supply the small monetary requirements of the country so soon after the numerous issues of Parákrama; but this can scarcely have prevented the new government from making at least a small issue in her honour, as has been done in the case of the other less important sovereigns.

[1] He points out (loc. cit. fig. 3) that one was engraved in the Asiatic Researches, and interpreted, doubtfully, by Professor Wilson, Ṣrí Ráma Náth.

56. श्री धर्म्माशोकदेव *Sri Dharmmáṣoka Deva.* Fig. 22.

The *r* is visible above the *m* in a few specimens only. It may be seen in the figure, which also gives a more complete form of the *d* than occurs on most of the specimens. The coin is very rare, like that of Wijaya Báhu, both these kings having reigned only twelve months. Dharmáṣoka was placed on the throne when he was three months old, though, as Prinsep slily remarks, 'the portrait would lead us to suppose him of mature age.' The well-preserved example figured is in my collection and weighs 65 grains.

57. श्री भुवनैकबाझ *Sri Bhuvanaika Báhu.* Fig. 16.

This sovereign came to the throne nearly a century after the last. His coins are not very rare, but good examples are seldom met with. I have only seen one or two which show the upper stroke of the diphthong *ai* or the vowel mark *u* distinct from the *bh*, which may account for Prinsep's reading Bhaváneka. The unusually well executed specimen in my collection, from which the figure is taken, weighs 63 grains.

58. I now come to coins whose classification is, at present, quite uncertain, and it is doubtful whether some of them belong to Ceylon at all; but I have thought it better to include them all in the plate for the purposes of comparison.

Fig. 24. Copper.

On the obverse the standing figure; on the reverse a bull, standing, to right; above it the new moon; to right of it the legend वी *Vi.* I think it is impossible with Prinsep, *loc. cit.*, to assign this very rare coin to Wijaya Báhu VI., who reigned in Ceylon as late as 1398 A.D., although he was also called Víra Báhu. Niṣṣanka Malla, A.D. 1187, in one of his inscriptions, calls himself, among other titles, Víra, and in another Víraràja; but his suzerainty was not acknowledged in India, and I doubt whether this coin has ever been found in Ceylon. Perhaps it may belong to Víra Páṇḍu, the prince whom Parákrama placed as his vassal on the throne of Páṇḍya (see above, § 38). The specimen figured is in the British Museum; it is the one described by Prinsep, and the only one known to me.

59. *The Lakshmi coin.* Figs. 9, 10. Gold.

On the obverse the standing figure as on the Lankeṣwara coin, but the ornament to the left above instead of below the arm, and to the right the trident. On the reverse the legend लच्मी *Lakshmi;* above it, the same symbol as on the obverse of Fig. 3; which symbol I take for the lotus. Fig. 9 in my collection weighs nearly 17 grains; Fig. 10 is in the British Museum, and weighs 16⅓ grains; these are the only specimens I know.

60. *The Tamraki coin.* Fig. 12. Gold.

Obverse the same as the last. On the reverse the legend *Tamraki* (?), with the lotus symbol above. From the specimen in the British Museum weighing 7·8 grains.

61. *The Iraka coin.* Fig. 13.

Obverse the same as the last, but the weapon (?) on the right is again held in, and not placed above, the hand. On the reverse the legend *Iraka* (?) surmounted by the lotus symbol, as in Fig. 4 with a stroke and dot behind it. The legend may possibly be Haraka or Daraka; if it could be read Laka, that would be the ancient Sinhalese form of Lanká. I have seen six or seven specimens of this coin, which is figured from one in my collection weighing 8 grains, and it has also been found in South India.

62. *The large Sétu bull coin.* Fig. 19. Copper.

On the obverse the standing figure as in the Lion coin, but the weapon or flower in the right hand has degenerated into a straight line with several cross-strokes. In the place of the lion the trisúla or trident, and a sceptre. On the reverse the bull sacred to Vishnu, above it the new moon with a star between the horns of the crescent; below, the legend சேது *Setu:* to the left of the figure five small dots, to the right twelve dots.

Prinsep's note on this coin is as follows:[1] 'Two of these exhibit a new type of reverse, the Indian bull Nandi, which may possibly betoken a change in the national religion. The legend beneath I immediately recognized as identical with the flourish on Fig. 12, turning the latter sideways to read it. What it may be is a more difficult question. The first letter bears a striking analogy to the vowel *e* of the Southern alphabets; but if so, by what alphabet is the remainder to be interpreted? for it may be equivocally read *betya, benya, chetya,* and perhaps *Chanda* or *Nanda.* The last alone is the name of a great conqueror in the Cholian and other Southern annals, but it would be wrong to build on so vague an assumption. It is at any rate probable that the "bull" device is a subsequent introduction, because we find it contained in the Halco Kanora coins below.'

63. I was for some time in doubt about the legend; but it now seems to me certain that the reading of the legend as above is correct. Sétu, which means originally a bridge or causeway, is used in the Bhagavata Purána as a name 'of Adam's Bridge or of one of the islands of this great group.' This latter can only be Rámeṣwaram, which is given as one of the meanings of the word in Winslow's Tamil Dictionary. Now we are distinctly informed in the Narendra-caritáwalokana-pradipikáwa, a very trustworthy Sinhalese epitome of the Mahávansa, that Parákrama's general Lankápura, after conquering Páṇḍya, remained some time at Rámeswaram, building a temple there, and that while on the island he struck *kahawanu,* that is kahápaṇas.[2] As the temple was built in honour of Vishnu, the bull need not surprise us, and it betokens no change in the national religion. It is true that Parákrama was a Buddhist, but the tolerance of Buddhist monarchs is well known, and one of the best preserved of the ruins of Parákrama's capital Pulastipura (the modern Topáre) is a Vimána for the worship of Vishnu. Round the outside of this building, which was erected either by Parákrama himself or by Niṣṣanka Malla, runs an inscription in Tamil characters of very much the same type as those on these Setu coins, and bearing the same relation to modern Tamil as the Sinhalese characters of Parákrama's and Niṣṣanka Malla's inscriptions do to modern Sinhalese. We shall, I hope, learn the purport of this inscription when Dr. Goldschmidt publishes his anxiously expected report on the Archæology of Ceylon: that the temple is sacred to Vishnu is certain from the four stone bulls on its summit, which are *couchant* like the bull on the coin. It will

[1] Loc. cit. p. 423.

[2] See my translation of the passage *loc. cit.* (§ 48, note 8).

be seen from my Dondra Inscription No. II.,[1] that this is not the only instance of Buddhist Kings in Ceylon building temples to Vishnu.

In dealing with coins that bear only a local description, there can seldom be absolute certainty in the identification, but—1. I know of no other ruler of Rameṣwaram of whom it is known from historical records that he struck coins there. 2. These resemble exactly in shape, size and appearance the Kahápaṇas struck by Parákrama in Ceylon. 3. As far as I have been able to ascertain, the South Indian coins are, with one exception,[2] of a quite different size, weight and appearance. 4. Those rájas who ruled over Rameṣwaram are not known to have issued any coins, while the Cholian and Páṇḍyan rájas who conquered it would not have had any particular reason to put Setu on their coins; whereas, to Parákrama, his continental conquests were naturally a source of more than ordinary pride. 5. If these coins belonged to any of the South Indian dynasty, they would probably bear some one of the constant symbols used by those dynasties on their coins. I regret very much that Sir Walter Elliot was not able to get ready his paper on South Indian coins for this series, before mine was published. With the very meagre accounts of South Indian numismatics at present obtainable, the Ceylon numismatist is working a good deal in the dark; but at present, and with the evidence before me, I think that these coins are probably the very ones referred to as having been struck by Parákrama's general Lankápura at Setu.

The coin is very rare, only five or six examples being known. My specimen, a very perfect one, from which the figure in the Plate is taken, weighs 68 grains.

64. *The small Sétu bull coin.* Fig. 18. Copper.

This is a half-size copy of the last, except that the large dots in the circle round the edge of the coin in Fig. 9 are here circles, and only three dots are required inside the circle to fill up the space by the side of the bull.

My own specimen and the one in the British Museum are the only ones known to me.

65. The exception referred to in the last paragraph but one is the coin with the inscription Rájarája (Fig. 8) which is inserted in the Plate, because it is the coin from which I believe the whole of the Ceylon series to be derived. Prinsep read it tentatively Gaja-rája,[3] and included it doubtingly in his plate of Ceylon coins. But the reading as above is no longer doubtful, and the coin has never, like those just mentioned, been found in Ceylon, while large numbers of the copper ones, and a few in gold, have been found in different places in South India, and especially in Amarávatí and Tanjúr. There were doubtless many princes in South India who arrogated to themselves the title of king of kings, and it became so much a mere name that one of the petty Cholian chiefs who opposed Lankápura is called Rája-rája Kalappa.[4] The title is also found used as an evident name in the copperplate grants of the Chálukya rájas in the eleventh century, though, as far as I know, it was never used alone.[5] Of course Parákrama, the conqueror of the Kings of Chola,

[1] Journal of the Ceylon Asiatic Society, 1873. [2] See next paragraph but one, § 65. [3] *Loc. cit.* p. 423.
[4] The India Office MS. of the Mahávansa, chap. 77, verse 75.
[5] Sir Walter Elliot informs me that there was a Rajaraja Chola circa 1022–1068, and a Rájarája Vikramáditya 1078.

Páṇḍya and Kalinga, and even of Rámánya and Kámboja, may well have called himself king of kings; but there can, I think, be no doubt that this coin belongs to one of the South Indian kings so called, and that it is the coin imitated by Parákrama in *his* coins, from which the Ceylon series is derived.

66. A coin of Niṣṣanka Malla has been referred to above (§ 48), of which only three examples are known, two in the possession of Sir Walter Elliot, and one in the collection of Mr. Dickson, Government Agent of the North Central Province, Ceylon. Unfortunately all three specimens are just now mislaid, and though this paper has been delayed in the hope that one would be found, we are at last compelled to go to press without being able to include a figure of this coin in the Plate. The coin is of copper, and exactly like Fig. 14, except as regards the legend on the reverse. This legend Mr. Dickson, in a paper read before the Numismatic Society on the 19th of May, 1876, conjectures may possibly be read *Sri Káli Gala Kija;* but he is unable to determine to what reign the coin may belong, and does not consider the above reading at all certain. Not having the coin before me, I speak with great diffidence; but it seemed to me, when I once had an opportunity of inspecting it, to bear the legend *Sri Kálinga Lankeṣvara.* Below the Ṣrí, which was the same as that of Fig. 14, I read

कालि

ग ल

क व

That the *anusvára* was not visible above the ग need not surprise us, as it was seldom visible on the Lankeṣwara coins (Figs. 1, 2, 3, 4); and on those coins we usually find simply Lakavara for Lankeṣvara, the dot for the anusvára, the small stroke for the *e*, and the tiny *ṣ* added above the *v*, being rarely legible. Lastly, throughout the series, when there are six letters below the *Ṣri*, the last of the six is almost always cut in half or quite missing, which would explain the absence of the *ra*.

If the reading I suggest should eventually prove to be correct, there can be very little doubt that the coin belongs to Niṣṣanka Malla. It is true that in the list of kings at § 45 it will be seen that there are five sovereigns, or six if Dharmáṣoka be included, who might have called themselves *Kálingan Lord of Ceylon;* but if the coins were struck by any successor of Niṣṣanka Malla, he would probably have used some title which would distinguish him from that prince, the first of those to whom the legend would be applicable. Of all the later Kálingan princes we have coins, except of Mágha, whe hated everything Sinhalese, and of Wikrama Báhu, who only reigned for three months. Kálinga Lankeṣvara is one of the titles used by Niṣṣanka Malla in his inscriptions,[1] and it is highly probable that he would imitate Parákrama the Great in his issue of coins, as he did in his inscriptions and his buildings.

					SECTION
67. For Figures	1–4	with legend	Ṣrí Lankeṣvara	see - -	46–48
,,	5, 6, 7	,,	Ṣrí Parákrama Báhu	,, - -	49
,,	8	,,	Rájarája	,, - -	65

[1] See above, § 48, note 8.

					SECTION.
For Figures	9, 10	with legend	Lakshmí (?)	see	59
,,	11	,,	Ṣrí Parákrama Báhu	,,	50
,,	12	,,	Taṁrakí (?)	,,	60
,,	13	,,	Iraka (?)	,,	61
,,	14, 15	,,	Ṣrí Parákrama Báhu	,,	51
,,	16	,,	Ṣrí Bhuvanaika Báhu	,,	57
,,	17	,,	Ṣrí Vijaya Báhu	,,	52
,,	18, 19	,,	Setu	,,	62, 64
,,	20	,,	Ṣrí Coḍaganga Deva	,,	53
,,	21	,,	Ṣrí Rája Lílávatí	,,	54
,,	22	,,	Ṣrí Dharmáṣoka Deva	,,	56
,,	23	,,	Ṣrímat Sáhasa Malla	,,	55
,,	24	,,	Ví . . .	,,	58
,,	25	Hook Money		,,	68–73

Hook Money.

68. There only remains to be mentioned *the hook money,* Fig. 25, which is comparatively a modern coin—if coin it can be called—but which is interesting from its curious shape and history.

The earliest mention of these silver hooks is by Robert Knox, who was kept prisoner for twenty years from 1659–1679 in the Kandian provinces of central Ceylon, and who after his escape published an account of his adventures and of the Sinhalese people. This most valuable work is thoroughly trustworthy. Knox and his companions were not confined in any prison, but in separate villages, where they were allowed to go in and out among the people. Most of them acquired property, and marrying Sinhalese women, became Sinhalese peasants; but Knox himself never gave up the hope of escape, and ultimately effected his purpose. His mode of life in Kandy was the best possible for gaining sure knowledge of the habits of the people; the simple straightforward style of his book must convince every reader of his truthfulness; and the more one knows of the state of society among the Sinhalese in remote districts who are little acquainted with Europeans, the more one learns to value the accuracy of his minute and careful observations. After mentioning the Portuguese copper "tangums," he adds: "There is another sort (of money) which all people by the king's permission may and do make; the shape is like a fish-hook, they stamp what mark or impression on it they please; the silver is purely fine beyond pieces of eight; for, if any suspect the goodness of the plate, is is the custom to burn the money in the fire, red hot, and so put it in water, and if it be not then purely white, it is not current money. The third sort of money is the king's proper coin; it is called a pounam (panam); it is as small as a spangle; 75 make a piece of eight, or a Spanish dollar; but all sorts of money are here very scarce, and they frequently buy and sell by exchanging commodities."[1]

[1] Edition by Philalethes, 4to. 1817, p. 197. The original work was published in 1681 by order of the East India Company.

69. While Knox was in captivity in Ceylon, Sir John Chardin was travelling through Persia, and he mentions that coins of silver wire had been made in Lari on the Persian Gulf, till that State was conquered by Abbas the Great of Persia (1582-1627); and that they were still much used 'en tout ce païs la, et aux Indes, le long du Golph de Cambays, et dans les païs qui en sont proche. On dit qu'elle avait cours autre fois dans tout l'Orient.'[1]

That the Ceylon coins were made in imitation of these is evident from the name given to them in another passage of Knox, where he says (p. 196) that two pælas of paḍi were sold in time of harvest for a *laree.*

70. If any confirmation were needed of Knox's statement that *laris* were actually made in Ceylon it would be found in a curious passage from the work of Pyrard, a Frenchman, who, fifty years earlier, had spent five years as a captive in the Maldive Islands, and who, after his escape, published a graphic and trustworthy account of the then habits and customs of the people there. Of their coinage he says (I quote the old French as it stands mostly unaccented): 'La monnoye du Royaume n'est que d'argent & d'une sorte. Ce sont des pieces d'argent qu'ils appellent *larins* de valeur de huist sols ou enuiron de notre monnoye, comme i'ay desia dit, longues comme le doigt mais redoublees. Le roy les fait battre en son isle & y imprimer son nom en lettres Arabesques.'

After saying that they received foreign coins, if of gold and silver, at their value by weight; and adding some general remarks on coinage in India, he goes on:

'Donc pour retourner, aux Maldives ne fait que des *larins*; d'autres pieces de moindre valeur ils ne s'y en fait point: tellement que pour l'effect de leur traffic ils coupent l'argent & en baillent un poids de la valeur de la marchandise achetee: ce qui ne se fait pourtant sans perte, car en coupant le larin on en perd la douzieme partie. Ils ne prennent piece d'argent qu'ils ne l'ayent pesee et mise dans le feu, pour en esprouuer la bonté. Aussi au lieu de billon & menuë monnoye ils usent de coquilles (cowries) dont i'ay cy-deuant touché quelque chose, & i'en parleray incontinent; les douze milles valent un larin.'[2]

71. So also Professor Wilson, in his remarks on fish-hook money in the Numismatic Chronicle,[3] describes some pieces of silver wire, not hooked, which were coined, in imitation of the old *laris*, at Bijapúr by Sulṭán 'Ali Ádil Sháh, who reigned from 1670–1691. They bear on both sides legends in Arabic characters; on one side the Sulṭán's name, on the other 'Zarb Lari Dangh Sikkha,' that is, 'struck at Lari, a stamped Dangh'—dangh being the name of a small Persian silver coin.[4] 'Traces of a date,' continues Professor Wilson, 'occasionally appear, but they are

[1] Voyages du Chevalier Jean Chardin en la Perse, second and complete edition, 4to. Amsterdam, 1835, vol. iii. p. 128. He travelled, according to the preface, from 1664–1677, and the first edition of his Voyages was published in 1717.

[2] According to Hamilton's Gazetteer, quoted by Mr. Thomas, 'Ancient Indian Weights,' cowries were worth in Bengal in 1820 rather less than 6000 for a rupee. The passage quoted is from the third edition of Pyrard's 'Voyages,' Paris, 8vo. 1619, pp. 248–250. From p. 5 it appears that he started in 1601; from p. 60 that he was wrecked on the Maldives on the 3rd July 1602. He escaped in 1607, and the first edition of his book appeared in Paris in 1611. Mr. Albert Gray, who gave me this reference, informs me that, from the words given by Pyrard, it is clear that the Maldivians are Sinhalese by race, though they are now Muhammadans by religion.

[3] Vol. xvi. pp. 179–182. These specimens are now in the British Museum.

[4] So Professor Wilson; Mr. Thomas informs me that 'struck *a* lari' would be a more precise rendering of the Persian words. [The so-called *Dangh* was primarily a *weight*, hence its equivalents, in silver, came to represent the fractions of the current coin.]

not very distinct, except in one instance, in which it may be read with some confidence 1071 = 1679 A.D. . . . . His (the Sulṭán's) retaining the designation of the place where this sort of money was originally fabricated is not without a parallel. . . . . The coins of the last Sháh Alam of Delhi, though coined all over India, continued to bear . . . . the mintage of Sháh Jehánabad; and the Company's rupee bore the legend "struck at Murshidabad," many years after it was coined at Calcutta. . . . . . . Mr. Coles mentions a document among the records of the Collectorate in which notice is given by the Government of Satara to the authorities of a place termed Kharaputtun of a grant of land of the *value of* 200 *Dhabal Larins,* which is dated 1711.[1] The fabrication of this money, extensively adopted by the last Bijapúr kings, was therefore continued by Sivaji, the founder of the Mahratta principality, and his successors. There is nothing in the appearance of the specimens brought from Ceylon to indicate an original fabrication.'

72. Of the original Larins of Laristán, none seem to be now extant; but it is quite clear, to use the words of Mr. Vaux,[2] that 'the Laristán coins having become, as Chardin says, popular in the East, they were extensively imitated;' and the testimony of Knox as to their having been made by private people in Ceylon must be accepted as true.

73. Professor Wilson says of the Bijapúr Larins that they are 'of the same weight (as the Ceylon hooks), viz. about 170 gr. troy.' But my specimen, from which the figure is taken, weighs only 74½ grains, and two others mentioned by Mr. Dickinson[3] weigh only 3 dwts. 2 gr., and 3 dwts. ½ gr. respectively. Authentic specimens from Ceylon are very rare. They have on one side only a stamp in imitation of Arabic letters, often clear enough, but of course quite illegible; and they are always hooked. I have not seen one with any marks which could be read Ṣrí in Sinhalese or Devanágarí characters, as suggested by Professor Wilson. How late these hooks were made in Ceylon it is impossible to state exactly; very probably until they were superseded by the Dutch coinage in the eighteenth century. They are known in Sinhalese literature under the name of *ridi,* i.e. silver; although this term was, doubtless, applied, before the introduction of the *Larins,* to other silver money, of which it is curious that no specimens should have survived. The term *ridi pahayi,* i.e. five ridis, is still used in remote districts in the sense of rix dollar.

[1] The Collectorate referred to is that of Ratnagiri on the coast of Canara. Mr. Coles had sent to the Government 396 *larins* found there in 1846, in digging the foundations of a house.

[2] Numismatic Chronicle, vol. xvi. p. 132.

[3] Ibid. p. 169.

APPENDIX TO PART IV. EUROPEAN CEYLON COINS.

74. No coins are known to have been struck by the Portuguese in or for Ceylon. Knox says (loc. cit.) that of three sorts of coins in use, 'one was coined by the Portugals; the king's arms on one side and the image of a friar on the other, and by the Chingulays called tangom massa. The value of one is ninepence English; poddi tangom or the small tangom is half as much;' but these were probably struck in Portugal, and not for use only in Ceylon.

75. The Dutch struck only a very few silver rix-dollars,[1] which are very rare, if not entirely extinct, and which I have never seen. A thick copper stuiver having on the obverse the monogram V.O.C. the O and C written over the sides of the V, and in the open part of the V the letter C, perhaps for Colombo or Ceylon, is occasionally met with. On the reverse is the legend 1 *Stuiver*, the numeral 1 being above the word *Stuiver* (which occupies the centre of the coin), and having four dots on each side of it. Below is the date, the dates in my collection being 1784, 1785, 1786, 1789, 1791, 1793, 1795. It is possible, however, that this C is only a mint mark, and that these coins, whose rough execution shows them to have been struck in the Dutch East Indies (the monogram V.O.C. stands for the initial letters of Vereinigte Ostindische Compagnie, *i.e.* United East Indian Company), were not, after all, struck in Ceylon. There are similar coins with two apparently Tamil letters below the words *stuiver*, and with T and G in the place of C.[2] If these letters stand for Trinkomalei and Galle, then one would expect Sinhalese letters, but they look like the Tamil letters I L, இ ல for Ilankei, the Tamil form of Lanká, that is, Ceylon.

76. The English have issued four types of coins besides the present one. Type 1, which is thick and coarsely executed, has on the obverse an elephant, below which is the date; on the reverse the words CEYLON GOVERNMENT running round a circle, within which is the value of the coin. Of this type there are three thick silver pieces (very rare) of the value of 96, 48, and 24 stuivers (4 of which = 1 fanam), weighing 280, 140 and 70 grains[3] respectively.[4] The 48 stuiver piece is equal to the rix dollar, and the three thick copper pieces of this type are respectively worth $\frac{1}{12}$, $\frac{1}{24}$, and $\frac{1}{48}$ of its value. These copper coins weigh 50 stuivers to the pound,[5] and are now difficult to procure.

Of this type, specimens of the following years, without letters, are in my collection, and those of the years marked (B.M.) are added from the British Museum collection:

Silver, 96 stuivers, 1808 (B.M.), 1809 (B.M.).
„ 48 „ 1803 (B.M.), 1804 (B.M.), 1808, 1809 (B.M.).
„ 24 „ 1803, 1804 (B.M.), 1808 (B.M.).

[1] Bertolacci, p. 79. [2] See Neumann's 'Kupfermünzen,' pp. 59, 60. [3] A florin weighs 174 grains.
[4] Bertolacci, pp. 88, 94, and 96. [5] Ibid. p. 90.

Copper, 4 stuivers, 1803 (B.M.), 1804, 1805 (B.M.), 1811 (B.M.), 1814, 1815.
„ 2 „ 1801, 1802, 1803, 1805 (B.M.), 1811, 1812 (B.M.), 1813 (B.M.), 1814, 1815, 1816.
„ 1 „ 1801, 1802, 1803, 1808 (B.M.), 1809, 1811 (B.M.), 1812, 1813, 1814, 1815, 1817.

77. Of Type 2 one issue was made, in copper, in 1802, of stuivers, half stuivers, and quarter stuivers; they are thin, like modern coins, and well executed, weighing 36 stuivers to 1lb.[1] Obverse and reverse as on the last type. The British Museum has specimens of this type dated 1804, but it is not certain whether these were ever in circulation.

78. Of Type 3 also only one issue was made, in 1815, of two-stuiver, stuiver, and half stuiver pieces in copper, and one issue of rix dollars in silver in 1821. Obverse of the copper, head of George III. to right, with legend GEORGIUS III. D. G. BRITANNIARUM REX: of the silver, head of Geo. IV. to left, with legend GEORGIUS IV. D. G. BRITANNIARUM REX F. D. Reverse of the copper, an elephant to left: above the legend, *Ceylon Two Stivers, One Stiver*, or *One-half Stiver*, with the date below. The silver the same, but the legend is *Ceylon one rix dollar*, and round the elephant is a wreath of flowers. The coins of this type are still occasionally met with in the bazárs, but the half stuiver is very difficult to get. Both this and the last issue were struck in England.

79. Lastly, Fanam pieces of two kinds were struck in silver. The first, which is very rare, and was issued about 1820, has simply round a small circle with a dot in its centre FANAM on the one side and TOKEN on the other, of a silver coin less than $\frac{3}{8}$ of an inch in diameter, and without date. The work-people who built Baddegama church, the oldest English Church in Ceylon, are said to have been paid in this coin, which is roughly executed. The other, which is half an inch in diameter, has on the obverse the bust of Victoria surrounded by the legend VICTORIA D. G. BRITANNIAR. REGINA F.D., and on the reverse the figures $1\frac{1}{2}$ and the date 1842, surmounted by a crown and surrounded by a wreath. This little coin, seldom met with in Ceylon, is beautifully executed, and was struck in England; whilst the *fanam tokens* were struck in Ceylon.

80. There is in the British Museum one silver specimen of another type, but whether this is a proof of an unpublished coin, or a specimen of a coin in actual circulation, I have been unable to ascertain. It has on the obverse the words TWO RIX DOLLARS in a square tablet surmounted by a crown; above it, CEYLON; below it on a scroll, DIEU ET MON DROIT, and below that again the word CURRENCY. On the reverse an elephant to the left, and below it the date 1812.

81. Bertolacci's rare work on Ceylon gives full details of the Dutch and English coinage down to the year 1815. He was Comptroller General of Customs in the island, and for some time acting Auditor General, and published his book after his return to England in London in 1817.

[1] Ibid. p. 87.

PART V. On the Ceylon Date of Gautama's Death.

82. Though not coming strictly within the limits of the present paper, a review of the conflicting evidence regarding the Buddhist era, which forms so important a date-point for all Indian chronologies, can scarcely be out of place in a work aiming at so much comprehensiveness and completeness as the 'Numismata Orientalia.' The present opportunity also chances to afford a fit occasion to meet the legitimate inquiries of those who have hitherto placed exceptional reliance on the value of the Ceylon annals, as preserved in their independent Páli and other local texts. At the request of Mr. Thomas, I have ventured, therefore, to add in this Part, a statement of the views on the general question at which I have arrived, and of the arguments by which they are supported, in amplification of a paper read before the Royal Asiatic Society in April, 1874.[1]

83. It is well known that, whereas, among the Northern Buddhists, there reigns the greatest uncertainty as to the date of the Buddha's death, the Southern Church is unanimous in fixing that event on the full-moon day of the month of Vaiṣákhá, that is, on the 1st of June, in the year 543 B.C. This latter date has been supposed the more worthy of credit as being found in very ancient writers, and as having formed the starting-point of a chronology in actual daily use among the Southern Buddhists; whereas the different dates of the Northern Churches are known to us only from modern writers,[2] and none of them have been made the basis of a chronological era.

84. It seems to me, however, that too much weight has been attached to this reasoning. As a matter of fact, it is very doubtful whether the Buddhist era has ever in any country been regularly and constantly used in every-day life as we use our era. Even in Ceylon the Buddhists, when Europeans first settled in the island, used, not only the Buddhist, but also and more frequently the Ṣaka era; and often dated events by neither, but merely by the year of the reign of the king in which the event occurred. Thus, of three comparatively modern inscriptions I have published, one is not dated at all, but gives the date of a previous gift as the year 2110 of the Buddhist

[1] See the report in the *Academy* of April the 25th in that year.

[2] Csoma de Körösi gives thirteen dates ranging from 2422 to 546 B.C. on the authority of a Tibetan work written in 1591; and another, 882 B.C., on the authority of an author who wrote in 1686.—'Tibetan Grammar,' p. 199. The more usual Chinese and Japanese date corresponds to 950 B.C. according to Rémusat (Foe Koue Ki, p. 79, where he gives the name, but not the date, of his Chinese authority); but on page 42 he mentions some other Chinese authors who place it in 609 B.C. See also Beal's valuable note in his Fa Hian, page 22, where twelve dates are given.

era (*Buddha-warshaya*);[1] a second is dated in the sixth year of the then reigning king;[2] and the third in the year 1432 of the 'auspicious and correct Ṣaka era' (*ṣri ṣuddha Ṣaka warusha*).[3] On the few occasions on which it was necessary to use a date, it was doubtless possible for the Ceylonese to calculate which year it was according to their *Buddha-warusha*; but the earliest record in which such an expression occurs is in a Pulastipura inscription of the twelfth century.[4] Before that time we have only the statements in the Dípavaṅsa and the Mahávaṅsa that Aṣoka's coronation took place 218, and the Council of Patna 236 years after Buddha's death; the chronology of those works being otherwise dependent entirely on the lengths of the episcopacy of the chief priests, and of the reigns of the kings. Turnour gives, in the introduction to his edition of the Mahávaṅsa, the dates of some other events dated in years of the Buddhist era, but he does not specify the authorities from which he draws his statements.[5] Before the Dípavaṅsa no instance has yet been found of the time of Buddhá's death being used as the starting-point from which to date events.

85. In this connexion it is at least worthy of notice that Fa Hian, who was in Anurádhapura in the year 412,[6] places in the mouth of an 'eloquent preacher' there, in an address urging the people to honour the Tooth, the statement that the Buddha had died 1497 years before—that is, in 1085 B.C.[7] Mr. Beal is in doubt whether this date, so strikingly at variance, both with the Ceylon date and that of other Chinese authors, should be ascribed to Fa Hian himself, or to the 'eloquent preacher'; but in either case it is strange that Fa Hian, who remained two years in the island,[8] should not, after his attention had been directed to the point, have acquired any better information than this as to the chronology then accepted there.[9] He probably filled up the date according to some Chinese calculation, when he drew up the account of his travels after his return home; but the passage is still very strange, especially as the Dípavansa was, almost certainly, already in existence (and even if not, at least the materials on which it is based) in the very Wiháre in which Fa Hian studied.

86. However this may be explained, it is clear that the Buddhist era was not used from the time at which it begins to run; and its accuracy depends, not on its having been constantly used, but *on the reliability of the calculations* made by those who first began to use it. In a similar manner our own era and the Hajra of the Muhammadans only began to be used a long time after the events from which they date; and, in reckoning back, the first calculators in each case made mistakes. We need not therefore be surprised to find mistakes in the calculation

[1] Ceylon Friend, 1870, p. 59. The probable date of the inscription is 1685.

[2] 'Journal of the Ceylon As. Soc.' 1870, p. 21. The king referred to is uncertain; and the date of the inscription either 1470 or 1540.

[3] Ibid. p. 26.

[4] In Parákrama the Great's Inscription on the *Gal Wiháre*. Comp. above, p. 24, note 1.

[5] Mahávansa, p. lx.

[6] See Rémusat's note, Foe Koue Ki, p. 347.

[7] Beal, p. 156; Rémusat, p. 335. The translations differ materially as to other points in the address, but agree in this.

[8] Beal, p. 165.

[9] That Fa Hian had had his attention called to the matter is evident from ch. vii. (Rémusat, p. 33; Beal, p. 22), where he fixes the death of Buddha in 'the time of Ping-wang of the Chau family.' The Chau dynasty is the third in the Chinese lists, and is quite legendary, as it fills up the period from 1118–252 B.C. (Numismatic Chronicle, vol. xvi. p. 53.) Ping-wang is said to have reigned from 770 B.C. to 720 B.C.

of an era that has been less regularly used, and began to be used only after a much longer interval; and we can place but very little reliance on any results, unless we know, and can check, the data on which they depend. It is in this respect that the Ceylon date is of so much more value than any other at present known; it is the only one which we can really test; and in Ceylon alone have such materials been preserved as enable us to make a calculation for ourselves.

87. The Ceylon date, as has just been pointed out, depends ultimately on two historical works, the Dípavaṅsa, Turnour's epitome of which, published in 1838, contains all the passages necessary for this discussion; and the first part of the Mahávaṅsa, edited by Turnour in 1837. The Dípavaṅsa is a history of Buddhism in India and Ceylon: the first eight books treating of India, the ninth and tenth of Ceylon previous to Devánampiya Tissa, the next six books of the events of that king's reign, and the last five of the kings of Ceylon for the next 500 years, B.C. 230—A.D. 302. As it is one of the books by 'ancient writers' mentioned by Mahánáma, the author of the Mahávaṅsa,[1] it must have been written some time before he wrote (which was between 460 and 470 A.D.), and may therefore be placed at the end of the fourth or beginning of the fifth century A.D.[2]

88. Neither of these works, of course, gives the date 543; but the Mahávaṅsa, as continued by subsequent writers, gives a succession of kings from the time of Aṣoka to the advent of Europeans in Ceylon, which fixes the date of Aṣoka's coronation in the year corresponding to the year 325 B.C. of our era, and both works place that event 218 years after the Buddha's death. The date 543 is found in fact to depend on three periods. 1st, the period from 161 B.C. to the present time, the calculation of which depends on the lengths of the reigns of the Ceylon kings down to the cession of the island to the English, and may be accepted as substantially correct. 2nd, a period of 146 years (Mahávansa, pp. 97, 162) from the accession of Duṭṭha Gámiṇi in 161 B.C. back to the accession of Devánampiya Tissa in the year of the Council of Patna, in the eighteenth year after Aṣoka's coronation. 3rdly, a period of 218 years (Dípavansa, 9th Bk.; Mahávansa, p. 22) from his coronation, or of 236 years from the Council back to the death of the Buddha (236+146+161=543). Accepting the first, I propose to examine at some length the two latter periods, as to which the Ceylon data—it will, I think, be found—are not reliable.

89. Adding 146 to 161, we obtain, according to the Mahávansa, the year 307 B.C. for Aṣoka's Council, and the year 325 therefore for his coronation, eighteen years before. Now on this point we have information from other sources, which, though it does not enable us to fix that event with absolute certainty within one year, is yet, as far as it goes, quite reliable. That information

[1] Turnour, p. 1. A stanza from it is quoted on p. 207.

[2] See *Jas. D'Alwis*, Attanugalu-vansa, pp. x, xxv. Descriptive Catalogue, pp. 118-168. *Turnour*, Journ. of the Bengal As. Soc. vol. viii. p. 922. *Weber*, Neueste Forschungen, p. 61; Indische Studien, vol. iii. p. 177; Review of Alwis's Pali Grammar (Engl. ed.), p. 24. *Westergaard*, Ueber Buddha's Todesjahr, p. 98 (of Prof. Stenzler's German edition). *St. Hilaire*, Journal des Savans, Fev. 1866, pp. 102, 113. *Max Müller*, Buddhaghosha's Parables, p. x, and Ancient Sanskrit Literature, p. 267. I am glad to say that my friend, Dr. Oldenberg, of Berlin, is now preparing a complete edition of the Dípavansa.

depends upon two ways in which Aṣoka is brought into connexion with European history; firstly through his grandfather Chandragupta, and secondly by his own Edicts.

90. Chandragupta, in Páli *Candagutta,* the Sandrokottas of the Greeks, is said to have had an interview with Alexander, who at the end of 326 B.C. was on the banks of the Hyphasis, and who left India in August, 325. Soon afterwards, but it is not exactly known how soon, Chandragupta became King of Magadha and of the whole Ganges valley, on the murder of King Nanda. After Alexander's empire fell to pieces, Seleukos Nikator fought with Chandragupta; and on peace being concluded, married his daughter, and sent as an ambassador to his court at Patna, then called Páṭaliputra, the celebrated Megasthenes, from whose lost book on India so much of the Western knowledge of India was derived. The date of these events is only known so far that they can be placed within a year or two of 306 B.C. So also the only passage which speaks of Chandragupta's accession to the throne does not give an exact date. Justinus says that Chandragupta had won the kingdom 'at that time when Seleukos was laying the foundations of his future power.'[1] Now Seleukos was Satrap of Babylon from 321-316; in that year he was compelled to fly to Egypt, where he remained four years. In 312 he returned with a small army; and so popular had he made himself during his former government, that in less than a year he drove out Antigonus; the Seleukidan era dating accordingly from 312 B.C. It follows, I think, that the passage in Justinus can only apply to the time when Seleukos was Satrap; and, therefore, if we can place implicit reliance upon the statement in question, that Chandragupta became king about 320 B.C.[2] He reigned, according to both Buddhist and Brahman authorities, twenty-four years,[3] and his son Bindusára twenty-five years according to the Buddhists, and twenty-eight years according to the Váyu Purána. As Asoka was crowned four years after the death of his father Bindusára, the date of his coronation would therefore fall either in 267 or in 264, according as we follow the Buddhist or the Purána statement of the length of Bindusára's reign.

91. We can fortunately check this result by an entirely independent calculation. In Aṣoka's thirteenth edict, which belongs to the twelfth year of his reign, he mentions five Greek kings as his contemporaries. Of this edict we have three copies, one from Kapur di Giri,[4] one imperfect one from Girnar (Giri-nagara),[5] and a third in good preservation from Khálsi.[6] It is agreed[7] that these five kings are

[1] Hist. Philip. xv. 4. The passage is as follows: *transitum deinde in Indiam fecit* [Seleucus], *quæ post mortem Alexandri, veluti cervicibus jugo servitutis excusso, præfectos ejus occiderat. Auctor libertatis Sandrocottus fuerat. . . . Sic adquisito regno Sandracottus ea tempestate, qua Seleucus futuræ magnitudinis fundamenta jaciebat, Indiam possidebat. . . . . .* Comp. *Pliny,* Hist. Nat. vi. 21, 68. *Diodorus Siculus,* xvii. 93. *Curtius,* ix. 2, 7. *Strabo,* i. 1; xv. 1, 11, 36. *Arrian,* Anabasis, v. 6, 2. Indica, v. 3, x. 5. *Plutarch,* Vita Alexandri, 62.

[2] On this point Westergaard's argument, Ueber Buddha's Todesjahr, pp. 115-117, seems to me quite convincing.

[3] The Váyu Purána quoted in Wilson's Vishnu Purána, p. 469, or vol. iv. p. 187, of Fitzedward Hall's edition. Dípavansa, Canto 5. Mahávansa, p. 21, where, by a copyist's blunder, 34 is given. Samanta Pasádiká (Buddhaghosha's commentary on the Vinaya), quoted by Turnour, Mah. p. lii.

[4] Cunningham's Archæological Report, vol. v. p. 20.

[5] Prinsep's Essays, vol. ii. p. 20, of Mr. Thomas's edition.

[6] Cunningham, in his Arch. Rep. vol. i. p. 247, gives the best text of this section of the Khálsi copy of the edict.

[7] Kern, Jahrtelling der zuidelijke Buddhisten, p. 27. Westergaard, Ueber Buddha's Todesjahr, p. 120. Cunningham in Thomas's Prinsep, vol. ii. p. 26. Lassen, Indische Alterth., vol. ii. p. 254.

1. *Antiochus* (Theos of Syria), 261-247.
2. *Ptolemy*(Philadelphus of Egypt), 285-246.
3. *Antigonus* (Gonatus of Makedon), 276-243.
4. *Magas* (of Kyrene), died 258.
5. *Alexander* (II. of Epirus), 272-254 (about).

92. The latest date at which these kings were reigning together is 258, the earliest 261; and if we could be certain that Aṣoka was kept informed of what happened in the West, we might therefore fix the twelfth year of his reign between these two years; and hence the date of his coronation between 270 and 273 B.C. This cannot, however, be done with absolute certainty. The inscription merely records that Aṣoka's regulations for planting trees on road-sides, for propagating rare medicinal plants, and for establishing hospitals for men and beasts, etc., had also been carried out in the dominions of the kings referred to.[1] We can, therefore, only draw the conclusion that in the twelfth year of his reign Aṣoka believed that these five kings had *lately* ruled in the West. The list indeed shows that his acquaintance with Western politics was not inexact. At the time in question the territories included within the limits of what had been Alexander's empire were in fact divided between the three kings whom he first mentions, and several lesser, but still independent, despots, such as the kings of Bithynia, Pergamum, and other unimportant States. The choice of the fourth and fifth of Aṣoka's list as representatives of these lesser States resulted probably from a reminiscence of the greatness of the celebrated Pyrrhus (the father of Alexander of Epirus), and of the intimate connexion between the Ptolemys and Magas of Kyrene,[2] of which Aṣoka may well have heard through the Greek embassies to his father, Bindusára. But it is unlikely that Aṣoka heard in 258 B.C. of the death of Magas in that year; and so unimportant had Alexander of Epirus become at the close of his life, that the date of his death is uncertain, and can only be approximately placed in 254, some thinking that it took place as early as 258. The language of the Edicts is, therefore, not inconsistent with their having been composed two or three or even more years after 258, which would bring down the date of Aṣoka's coronation a corresponding number of years after 270 B.C.

93. These considerations, however, are sufficient to show that the Indian tradition of the length of the interval between Chandragupta's and Aṣoka's coronations are not incorrect; and that we cannot be far wrong, on the double ground of the Greek notices of Chandragupta and of the Aṣoka Edicts, in placing the latter in or about the year 265 B.C.—say, for certain, between 260 and 273 B.C. That this date is at least approximately correct is sufficiently evident from

[1] Compare also the second edict of Girnar; of which the best text will be found in Kern, Jahrtelling, etc., pp. 89 and foll. This is, of course, only a royal boast.

[2] Magas was a step-son of Ptolemy Soter, being the son of his accomplished and beautiful wife Berenike by a former husband. Magas conquered Kyrene with an Egyptian army (B.C. 308), and was at first only Viceroy under Ptolemy Soter, whose daughter he married; but on Soter's death in 280, he asserted his independence, and even fought against Ptolemy Philadelphus. On peace being concluded, the daughter of Magas, also called Berenike, was betrothed to Ptolemy's son Euergetes.

the consensus of scholars on the point. Professor Lassen estimated it at 263 B.C.;[1] Professor Max Müller at 259 B.C.;[2] Professor Westergaard places it either in 264 or in 268 B.C.;[3] while Professor Kern makes it 270 B.C.[4]

94. The Ceylon chronicles, however, place that event, as we have seen above (§ 89), in the year corresponding to 325 B.C. of our era; they are therefore certainly in error to the extent of 60 years or thereabouts. We have discovered this error by a comparison with European history; but it is instructive to notice that it might also have been discovered, if not so accurately corrected, by a careful study of the Ceylon chronicles themselves. We find, namely, in the period between the accession of Devánampiya Tissa, the contemporary of Aṣoka, and the accession of Duṭṭha Gámiṇi in 161 B.C., some very curious details. Tissa himself is said to have reigned 40 years, and after his death three of his brothers reign successively for just ten years each; two Draviḍian usurpers then reign for 22 years; and after them a fourth brother of Tissa's for just ten years more. The latter commenced his reign therefore 92 years after the death of his father, Muṭa Síwa; and as the latter had reigned for 60 years, we have only two generations to fill up a period of 162 years! After the fourth brother another Draviḍian usurper reigns for double 22, that is 44 years; and to make it quite sure that we have not misunderstood Mahánáma in these numbers, it should be added that he himself gives the sum of these reigns at 146 years,[5] which is the correct total of the above numbers.

95. But not only is this period on the face of it incorrect, and incorrect by being too long; the very chronicle, by the details which it gives, points out one way in which the mistake may have, partly at least, arisen. It states that Mahinda and his sister Sanghamittá were admitted into the Buddhist Order of Mendicants in the sixth year of their father Aṣoka's reign,[6] and were then respectively 20 and 18 years old;[7] that they came to Ceylon 12½ years afterwards; and that they died there at the ages of 60 and 59, in the eighth and ninth years respectively after Devánampiya Tissa's death.[8] It follows that Mahinda was 32½ years old when he came to Ceylon; and that he lived in the island 27½ years, of which eight years were subsequent to Tissa's death. Tissa died therefore 19½ years after Mahinda's arrival, and he began to reign half a year before. His whole reign therefore was, according to these data, 20, and not, as given in the chronicle,[9] 40 years.

96. The manner in which the Ceylonese scholars have got over this difficulty is worthy of notice. Turnour, doubtless depending upon them, and upon the Mahávansa Ṭíká, translates the passages referring to the deaths of Mahinda and his sister as if the text had, not in the 60th and

[1] Indische Alterthumskunde, second edition, vol. ii. pp. 60–62.

[2] History of Ancient Sanskrit Literature, p. 298.

[3] Oversigt over det kongelige danske vidensk bernes selskabs Forhandlinger i Aaret, 1860; p. 122 of the German translation entitled Ueber Buddha's Todesjahr, Breslau, 1862.

[4] Over de Jaartelling der zuidelijke Buddhisten, Amsterdam, 1873, p. 27.

[5] Turnour, pp. 97, 162.

[6] Mahávansa, p. 37. From page 34 indeed it would appear that this ought to be seven, not six; for Sumana was ordained in the fourth year, the building of wiháras occupied three years, and then the ordination of Mahinda took place (p. 35, last line). But see below, § 114.

[7] Ibid. p. 36.

[8] Ibid. pp. 124, 125. Turnour's rendering sixty-nine in the latter case is a mere slip.

[9] Ibid. p. 124. This discrepancy was first pointed out by Westergaard.

59th year of their age, but in the 60th and 59th year *after their ordination*; regardless of the fact that if this interpretation be right, the correct number for Sanghamittá would be 61, and not 59 (12 years before Tissa's accession, 40 during his reign, and 9 years afterwards). But the text has distinctly 60 and 59 (*saṭṭhi-vasso* and *ekúna-saṭṭhivassá*) years old: and though the Dípavansa, in a passage referring to the same subject,[1] confirms the use of the word *vasso* in the sense here adopted by Turnour and his pandits; it is clear that we have, in these data, a confusion between the natural and what I would venture to call the spiritual age of Mahinda and his sister.

97. There is, therefore, both internal and external evidence that this period of 146 years is too long; and it must be corrected to bring it into accord with the more trustworthy information which places Aṣoka's coronation at 265 B.C. or shortly after.

98. But if the Ceylon date for Aṣoka is placed too early in the Ceylon chronicles, can we still trust the 218 years which they allege to have elapsed from the commencement of the Buddhist era down to the time of Aṣoka? If so, we have only to add that number to the correct date of Aṣoka, and thus fix the Buddhist era at 483 B.C. or shortly after. Of the answer to this question there can, I think, be no doubt. We can not: for though we have here no external evidence to guide us, the internal evidence, the very lists of the kings and priests whose reigns or patriarchates amount to the period of 218 years, gives sufficient proof that it, also, is too long. But I venture to think that in this period enough details have been preserved to enable us, from internal evidence alone, to ascertain within a few years the extent of the error, and thus to arrive approximately at the true date of Gautama's death.

99. The Dípavansa bases its chronology chiefly on the succession of Theras, the Heads or Chiefs of the Buddhist Order of Mendicants (*Thera-paramparā*); and also gives chronological details regarding the succession of the Kings (*Rája-paramparā*) of Magadha and of Ceylon. The Mahávansa bases its chronology on the succession of the Kings, and gives isolated details regarding the succession of the Theras. The following is the list of the Kings of Magadha as given in the Mahávansa:[2]—

[1] In Bh. xvii., where it says of Mahinda,

Paripuṇṇa-dvádasa-vasso Mahindo ca idhágato
Saṭṭhi-vasse paripuṇṇe nibbuto Cetiya-pabbate.

In Childers's Dictionary, under Vasso, the reference to the passage 'paripuṇṇa-vísati-vasso having completed twenty-one years,' should be Dickson's Upasampadá-Kammavácá, p. 4, and twenty-one is a slip for twenty, arising from the confusion between being twenty-one years old, and having completed the twentieth year of one's age. See below, § 114.

[2] Turnour's edition, pp. 10, 15, 21, tabulated on p. xlvii. Comp. Dípavansa, book v., at the end, where Káḷasoka is omitted, and his ten sons made brothers of Susunága; whilst at the commencement of the same book Aṣoka is mentioned as the son of Susunága.

KINGS OF MAGADHA.

1. Bhátiya, in whose reign Gautama was born.
2. Bimbisára; reigned fifteen years before Gautama as the Buddha visited Rájagriha.

	reigned	37	years	afterwards
3. Ajátasattu	,,	8	,,	before the Buddha died, and
	,,	24	,,	afterwards.
4. Udáyi-bhaddaka	,,	16	,,	
5. Anuruddhaka } 6. Muṇḍa }	,,	8	,,	between them.
7. Nága-dásaka	,,	24	,,	
8. Susunága	,,	18	,,	A new dynasty.
9. Káḷasoka	,,	10	,,	before the Second Council and
		18	,,	afterwards.
10. His ten sons	,,	22	,,	A new dynasty.
11. The nine Nandas	,,	22	,,	,,
12. Chandagutta	,,	24	,,	
13. Bindusára	,,	28	,,	
14. Aṣoka	,,	4	,,	before his coronation.
TOTAL		218	years	between Gautama's death and Aṣoka's coronation.

100. We shall return to the consideration of this list presently.[1] But I would here add that Nos. 3, 4, 5, 6, and 7 are said to have each murdered their father and predecessor; and I would also draw attention firstly to the frequent recurrence of multiples of 4 and 8 in the numbers, and to the curious coincidence in the numbers assigned to the two dynasties, Nos. 10 and 11, each of which is said to have reigned 22 years; and secondly to the fact that the Sanskrit authorities have also preserved for us in the Puránas a list of the Kings of Magadha during this period, containing names identical with some of the above, but omitting others, and generally shorter in its arrangement.

101. The following is the list from the Mahávansa of the Kings of Ceylon, the numbers in brackets referring to the pages of Turnour's edition, on which the details are given :—

[1] Below, § 110.

KINGS OF CEYLON.

1. Wijaya who reigned -	38	years after Gautama's death (p. 53).	
Interregnum - - -	1	,,	(p. 54).
2. Paṇḍu-wása Dewa - -	30	,,	(p. 58). Son of the last (p. 54).
3. Abhaya - - - - -	20	,,	(p. 63). Son of the last (p. 57).
Interregnum (Tissa, p. 63)	17	,,	(6 on p. 62; 4 on p. 63; 7 on p. 64).
4. Paṇḍukábhaya - - -	70	,,	(p. 67). Nephew of the last (pp. 56, 59, 60).
5. Muṭa Síwa - - -	60	,,	(p. 68). Son of the last (p. 67).
TOTAL - - -	236	,,	from Gautama's death to the accession of Devánampiya Tissa in the 18th year of King Aṣoka.

102. In this list we have only five Kings, each the son or nephew of his predecessor, to fill out a period of 236 years. Half that time would be a long average. Paṇḍukábhaya was 37 years old when he began to reign (p. 67; and comp. p. 58); he must, therefore, have been 107 years old when he died. He married his cousin, Suvaṇṇa-pálí, before the interregnum began (p. 62); so that their son, Muṭa Síwa, must have died 147 years after his parents' marriage. To show how little these figures can be depended upon, further comment would be needless; but it is worthy of notice for other reasons also that the two interregnums amount to just 18 years—the exact difference between the total of this list and the total of the last. To obtain this number, the six years on p. 62, which elapsed before Abhaya was deposed, are nevertheless included in the second interregnum; and in the Dípavansa (book iv.), the 10th year of the Magadha King Nágadása is said to be the same as the 20th of the Ceylon King Paṇḍu, which presupposes the omission of the first interregnum. It is probable that the interregnums are an afterthought; and that the list was first arranged to fill up the period of 218 years appearing in the list of Magadha Kings.

103. Passing now to the *Thera-paramparà*, it should first be noticed that a number of details regarding the Theras are dated in such and such a year of such and such a King, either of Magadha or of Ceylon; whilst other figures are given without reference to the Kings. Reducing the former, on the basis of the above lists of the Rája-paramparà, to the era of Buddha, we have the following result:[1]—

LIST OF THE THERAS,

INCLUDING THE DETAILS DATED BY THE KINGS.

Name.	Date of Birth.	Date of full Admittance to the Order.	Age at full Admittance of Successor.	Length of Membership.	Age at Death.	Date of Death.
Upáli	44 Bef. B.	..	60	..	74	30 A.B.
Dásaka	14 A.B.	16 A.B.	40	50	64	80 A.B.
Sonaka	60 A.B.	59 A.B.	40	44	66	124 A.B.
Síggava	100 A.B.	100 A.B.	64	55	76	176 A.B.
Tissa	158 A.B.	164 A.B.	66	68	86	234 A.B.
Mahinda	204 A.B.	224 A.B.		60	89	285 A.B.

[1] Dípavansa; Bhánavára iv. verses 38 and foll.; Bh. v. last 30 vv.

104. This list will no more bear examination than the last. That Siggava was admitted to full orders in the year in which he was born appears clearly on the face of the table, other absurdities are only slightly latent, and Turnour has already pointed out more than enough.[1] 'Manifestly,' says Mr. Turnour, speaking especially of the Siggava details, 'these dates also are an imposition.' It does not seem to have occurred to him that his own mode of calculation (on the basis just referred to) might possibly, seeing that it came to so absurd a conclusion, be the cause of the absurdity. Let us, however, try how the list looks if we leave out all those dates which depend on the lists of Kings, and take only those data which are stated absolutely without any reference to the Rája-paramparà. We shall then have from the Dípavansa the following

LIST OF THE THERAS,

INDEPENDENT OF THE LISTS OF KINGS.

Name.	Age when he admitted his successor to full Membership.	Age when he died.	No. of years he was full Member of the Order.	Years during which *both* he and his Successor were full Members of the Order.	Years of his full Membership *before* his Successor's admission to full Membership.
Upáli	60	74	..	..	..
Dásaka	45	64	50	19	31
Sonaka	40	66	44	26	18
Siggava	64	76	55	12	43
Tissa	66	86	68	20	48
			217		140
Dásaka was admitted to full Membership - - - - - - -					16 A.B.
The Second Council was in the twelfth year of Mahinda's full Membership					12
Date A.B. of Aṣoka's Council - - - - - - - - - - -					168
					18
Date A.B. of Aṣoka's coronation - - - - - - - - - -					150

105. Only the data of the former three of these five columns are actually found in the Dípavansa; the two latter being calculated from them. The text, for instance, says that Sonaka was 66 years old when he died; that he had then been ordained to the *upasampadá* degree for 44 years; and that he was 40 years old when he received Siggava into full membership,—or, in other words, when he, at the *Upasampadá Kammavácá*, or Ordination Ceremony, at which Siggava received the *upasampadá* degree, filled the position of *upajjháya* or superior. It follows that for the remaining 26 years of his life both he and Siggava were full members of the order, and that 18 years had elapsed since he himself had received the *upasampadá* ordination, Dásaka then acting as *upajjháya*. In the same way it is found that 31 years elapsed between the ordination of

[1] Journal of the Bengal Asiatic Society, vol. viii. pp. 919–933, v. and especially 923. Turnour's MS. was incorrect in some places. Thus, in the numbers which concern us here, 17, at p. 929, line 22, should be 14; 5, at p. 930, line 4, should be 55; and 80, at p. 930, line 25, should be 86, according to the MS. of the Dípavansa presented by the King of Burma to the Colombo Government Library, the best MS. of the Dípavansa I know of.

Dásaka, in the 16th year after Gautama's death, and the ordination of Sonaka; 43 years between the ordinations of Siggava and Moggali-putta Tissa; and 48 years between those of Tissa and Mahinda. These figures added together make 156 (16+31+18+43+48) for the number of years which elapsed, according to this Thera-parampará, between Gautama's death and the ordination of Mahinda; and Mahinda having been ordained in the 6th year after Aṣoka's coronation, it follows that the dates 150 A.B. for that event, and 168 A.B. for the Council of Patna, are the only dates consistent with this list.

106. It will thus be seen that *the very oldest of the Ceylon historical books gives numbers which only allow for* 168 *years having elapsed between the death of the Buddha and Aṣoka's council, and for* 150 *years between the death of the Buddha and Aṣoka's coronation.* But the same book (Dípavansa, 9th canto, last lines) says that the council was held 236 A.B., so that the coronation was 218 A.B. Which, if either, of the two dates is the correct one?

107. There can be no doubt, I think, but that the shorter period is, at least, the more correct; for, quite apart from the lists of Kings, and judging only from the list of Theras, the number of Theras succeeding one another is not long enough to fill out 236 years, whereas they could well have occupied the shorter period. We have seen also above that the lists of Ceylon Kings cannot possibly fill out the whole of the 236 years; and though the list of the Magadha Kings contains nothing which would show, from internal evidence alone, that it is too long; it is longer than the corresponding list preserved by the Brahmin authorities.

108. The shorter period must therefore be held to overrule the longer one; can it also be considered as itself correct? To this the answer can only at present be given on a balance of probabilities. To me it seems very natural that Mahinda, the son of Aṣoka, should have taken for his *upajjháya*, or superior, the most influential and important Thera in the Order; and that the names of *his* superiors and teachers, and of *their* superiors, should be well known. It is also not at all improbable that the ages of these men at their death should have been remembered, since it is an important part of the recognized service at the admission to the *upasampadá* degree, that the ages of the candidates should be then recorded; and by that record the monk's precedence, at every subsequent meeting of the Order, is determined.[1] The evidence is not, therefore, in favour of these numbers having been invented, like those of the list of Ceylon Kings; but rather the contrary. On the other hand, however, they may, of course, contain mistakes; one figure at least which would affect our result must be considered unreliable until better MSS. shall enable us to correct the existing text;[2] and concerning one figure which would not affect the result there are various readings in the MSS.[3] From Mahinda's time to that of the author of the Dípavansa there was an unbroken succession of teachers and

[1] Dickson's Upasampadá Kammaváćá, p. 5, and p. 14, note *e*, of the separate edition, or J.R.A.S., June, 1873.

[2] The length of Dásaka's upasampadáship (50 years) is inconsistent with the age at which he died (64 years). It cannot be more than 44, as he must have been 20 years old when he was ordained. There must be an old error in the number 50, but the error cannot be large.

[3] The age of Tissa at his death is given twice, by all MSS. except one, at 80; but in one passage our best MS. reads 86 (Dip. Bh. V. vv. 86, 98. (See above, note 1, § 104.) As he was 66 in the 6th year of Aṣoka, and died in the 26th, this last must be right. But the interval of twenty years between Mahinda's ordination and Tissa's death (the important figure for our calculation) is independent of the verses cited.

students, of writers and readers. The works composed during the interval are only known to us through Buddhaghosha's commentaries which took their place, just as in Ceylon the Mahávansa took the place of the Dípavansa. The latter has only been preserved to us by the fortunate chance that when Buddhaghosha left Ceylon for Burma, the Mahávansa had not yet been written; all the Ceylon MSS. of the Dípavansa being derived mediately or immediately from Burma. And as, if it had been lost, we should have known of it only from the Mahávansa, so we know the names only of the different commentaries and treatises which existed before Buddhaghosha; such as the Andha Aṭṭhakathá, the Mahá Aṭṭhakathá, the Múla Aṭṭhakathá, the Mahá Paccarí, the Kurundi, the Budha Aṭṭhakathá, the Saṅkhepa Aṭṭhakathá, etc. These, however, are enough to show that the Thera-parampará had every chance of being carefully preserved during the period between Mahinda and the author of the Dípavansa. At the present stage of our discussion we may conclude, I think, that we have in this list the actual names of the Thera-parampará from Gautama to Mahinda; whether the aggregate period assigned to them can be taken as correct, we shall be better able to judge after some further remarks.

109. If the names, to say nothing of the numbers, of the succession of Theras recorded in the earliest Ceylon histories are consistent only with a shorter date, how is it that the authors of those books have made the mistake which certainly lies in the dates 236 A.B. and 218 A.B., assigned in them to the Council of Páṭaliputra, and to the coronation of Asoka? This is, of course, very difficult to answer; for while the number of ways in which a right calculation can be made is limited, the number of ways in which a mistake may be made is very large. Still some light may be thrown, I think, even on this.

110. The larger date is 218 A.B., the shorter 150 A.B. The difference is 68 years. Now in turning back to the list of the Kings of Magadha, the reader will discover the curious coincidence that the reigns of the Susunága dynasty amount in the aggregate to just 68 years. 'That may be only chance,' says the careful reader. Very good: but on examining the list of Ceylon Kings he will find precisely this period of 68 years re-appearing from the beginning of one interregnum to the end of the other. It is a very strange chance that this particular period should stand in *both* lists divided by clear and distinct lines from the rest of the chronology. But this is not all. We have no other list of Ceylon Kings with which to compare ours; but we have another list of the Magadha Kings drawn up from Hindu authorities, by Professor Wilson in his edition of the Vishnu Purána.[1] In the Hindu list we find the very Susunága dynasty referred to in the last paragraph *separated* from the other names, and placed *before* the rest of the Kings corresponding to those in the Ceylon list.[2] And, finally, if we treat the Ceylon list in a similar manner, and place the Susunága dynasty before the others, we obtain a new list remarkably in agreement with that of the Puránas.

[1] Vishnu Purána, pp. 466 and foll.; or vol. ix. pp. 180-188 of Fitzedward Hall's edition of Prof. Wilson's works.

[2] The same dynasty is also omitted in the Jain lists given by Dr. Bühler (*Indian Antiquary*, Dec. 1873, p. 363), but as that list also omits all the other kings down to the Nandas, it does not throw any light on this question.

The correctness of this statement will, perhaps, be most easily proved, by arranging the lists in parallel columns—an arrangement which will also throw light on the forms of several of the names.

List of the Magadha Kings from the Puránas.[1]	Váyu	Matsya.	List of the Magadha Kings from the Ceylon Chronicles (re-arranged).	
Ṣiṣunága	40	40	*Susunága*	18
Kákavarṇa[2]	36	36	*Káḷasoka*[2]	28
Kshema-dharman	20	36	*His ten sons together*	22
Kshatra-ujas[3]	40	36	Bhátiya[3]	10
Bimbisára	28	28	Bimbisára	52
Ajátaṣatru	25	27	Ajátasattu	32
Dharbaka[4]	25	24	Udaya-bhadraka[4]	16
Udayáṣva[4]	33	33	Anuruddhaka }	8
Nandi-vardhana	42	43	Muṇḍa }	
Mahá-nandin	40	42	Nágadásaka	24
Nanda and his son	83 and	12	9 Nandas	22
Chandragupta	24	..	Chandagutta	24
Vindusára	25	..	Bindusára	28
Aṣokavardhana	4	..	Dhammásoka	4

111. If the Páli and Sanskrit lists had been derived from similar sources, and the Páli one afterwards altered, by a change in the relative position of the first three items in the above list, in order to make the interval between Gautama's death and Aṣoka's coronation longer by 68 years, all the above coincidences would be explained. Now it will have been noticed that the last two columns in the table above (§ 104), from which we obtained the shorter date, are calculations not found in the Dípavansa. Is it possible that the Ceylon chronicler should have forgotten to make those subtractions? *In other words, that they added up not the years which elapsed between* each ordination and the next, but the years during which each Thera was full member of the Order (*upasampanno*) ; forgetting that *in the earlier part* of each Thera's upasampadáship the previous Thera's upasampadáship *was still running*.

112. We have seen above (§ 96), that a similar confusion was actually made between the natural and the spiritual ages of Mahinda and his sister ; and there is another consideration that strongly supports the probability of this mistake having been made. While each of these Theras did actually receive upasampadá, and the date of his having received it was carefully recorded, none

[1] The Puránas from which this list has been made are the Vishnu, Váyu, Matsya, and Bhagavata Puránas. They agree in the number and order of the kings, but differ slightly in several of the names. Only the above give the lengths of the reigns. I have followed the forms of the names adopted by Lassen in his Indische Alterthumskunde, vol. i. p. xxxiii, and vol. ii. p. 1207.

[2] Both kákavarṇa and káḷa mean "black." It is quite impossible with Kern, Jahrtelling, p. 4, to take the latter in the sense of 'chronological.' See Childers's Dict. under "Káḷo," and p. viii, note 4 ; Westergaard, p. 126. It is the latter, not the former, part of the name which has been changed.

[3] The Sanskrit form suggests the reading Khattiya ; but the above form occurs not only in Mahávansa Tíká (T., p. 10), but also in the Dípavansa, canto iii.

[4] The Páli name corresponds here to the two Sanskrit ones. Of these, Dharbaka, a form found nowhere else, is probably metathesis for Bhadraka ; and the aṣva of Udayáṣva does not appear in the Matsya Purána.

of them in point of fact can have become Chief of the Vinaya, or Chief of the Order, in any patriarchal sense; and even the date of 218 A.B. for the coronation of Aṣoka is derived from adding up, not the years of their chiefship of the Vinaya, but the years of their upasampadáship. Yet during the whole account great stress is laid on the fact that each of these Theras was *Vinaya-pámokkha*, which has all the while nothing to do with the chronology. Now the Primacy of each Thera, unlike his upasampadáship, would have begun where the last one ended; so that if a confusion had been made between the two, the mere addition of the numbers, without subtraction, would have followed as a matter of course. The chronicler would then have argued thus: Tissa is Mahinda's superior (*upajjháya*), Siggava was Tissa's superior, and so on back to Gautama; if I add together the years of upasampadáship of these superiors back to Dásaka, who was alive when Gautama died, I shall find out the full time that has elapsed since Gautama; but Mahinda was not ordained at the time of Aṣoka's coronation, so I must leave him out. He would then have *added up the third column* in the table at § 104 *instead of the fifth*; and would have concluded that 217 years had elapsed between the time of Gautama and Aṣoka's coronation.

113. It is not a sufficient objection that this would have been too foolish to be possible. If not this, then the chroniclers made some other mistake as bad or worse.[1] May the writer venture to ask, was not the reader somewhat puzzled at first sight by the headings of the columns in the table at § 104? For himself, the writer is willing to confess that he does not find the argument they contain by any means so simple as it is undeniable; and if further proof were needed, it would be found in the fact that it does not seem to have occurred to Mr. Turnour, or Professor Westergaard, or Professor Kern.

114. A more valid objection seems to be, that the mistake would then have been 67 instead of 68 years, as we have found that it actually was. But this does not follow. Moggali-putta Tissa was ordained in the fourth year of Aṣoka.[2] At a festival three years afterwards Aṣoka determines on the ordination of Mahinda;[3] yet immediately afterwards it is said that Mahinda was ordained in the sixth year of Aṣoka.[4] So again, though the coronation of Aṣoka had been fixed in the year 218 A.B., and the Council of Patna in the 17th year of Aṣoka,[5] yet the Council is placed in 236 A.B. Once more, an event placed in the 16th year of King Bimbisára is in the following sentence said to have happened when 15 years of his reign had elapsed.[6] Again, in the same page of the Mahávansa it is said that Bimbisára reigned 37 years 'after his conversion,' but in the Sinhalese authorities, from which Spence Hardy drew his account, the same thing is meant when it is said that 'he rendered assistance to Buddha during 36 years.'[7] This last instance

[1] The mistake may also have arisen from the confusion between Kákavarṇa and the Aṣoka under whom they place the 2nd Council: but there are many difficulties in working out this explanation. The confusion seems to me a result, not a cause, of the mistake; and it is a confirmation of my view that Táranátha, the Tibetan historian, while placing the Council, like every one else, under an Aṣoka, says that the assembled monks were fed by Nanda (p. 41). According to my rectification, the 2nd Council falls under Chandragupta. It is a very common error to suppose this Council unknown to Northern Buddhists. The question is too long to be discussed in a note, but see my '*Buddhism*,' pp. 215 to 221, and 226.

[2] Mahávansa, p. 34. [3] Ibid. pp. 34, 36.

[4] Ibid. p. 37. [5] Ibid. p. 42. [6] Ibid. p. 10.

[7] Hardy's Manual of Buddhism, page 193; and compare Bigandet's 'Life or Legend of Guadama,' p. 249.

explains the way in which these differences of one year, which are not infrequent, have arisen; and if our calculators had once concluded that 217 years had elapsed between the death of Buddha and the coronation of Aṣoka, they would also have expressed the same thing by saying that it took place in the 218th year after that event. A difference of one year would not therefore be a discrepancy fatal to the proposed explanation; but even this slight difference depends on our placing the Council in the 18th year of Aṣoka according to the more numerous authorities. As has been just pointed out, the Mahávansa itself places it, in one passage, in the 17th year of his reign; and if we had used 17 instead of 18 in our calculation, there would have been no discrepancy at all.

115. The foregoing examination would seem to show that the persons who first calculated the dates 218 and 236 A.B. (perhaps the earlier chroniclers themselves) had as data to work upon the tradition regarding the succession of the Kings of Magadha, and the tradition regarding the succession of Theras from Gautama to Mahinda (including the numbers in the table in § 104)—traditions which had been brought by Mahinda to Ceylon. They had also certain details regarding the succession of Kings in Ceylon, including the names, but probably not the numbers, given in the table at § 101. It is almost certain that they had not before them the numbers given in the table at § 110 from the Váyu and Matsya Purânas. In reckoning backwards *they used the Thera-parampará*; and in doing so they made some arithmetical blunder—very likely the blunder I have suggested; and thus carried the dates further back than the very numbers before them, which they have fortunately preserved, would rightly warrant.

116. Either they themselves, or some later chronicler,—for the chronology preserved to us is probably due to more than one mind,—then noticed the discrepancy between the dates thus wrongly derived from the Thera-parampará, and those of the Rája-parampará of Magadha. They concluded that the latter, to them the less sacred of the two, must be wrong; and they accordingly harmonized the two lists by bringing the Susunága dynasty down into that part of the list embracing the period to which the dates 218 and 236 refer.

117. Before the Dípavansa was written also, the belief in the curious tradition, of which no trace is found in the Parinibbána Sutta, assigning the date of Wijaya's landing to the exact time of Gautama's death,[1] must have become fixed. It followed that from that time to the accession of Devánampiya Tissa 236 years must have elapsed; and the Rája-parampará of Ceylon was brought into agreement with that belief by assigning to the Kings whose names had been handed down reigns of the length whose impossibility has been fully shown above (§ 102); regardless of the fact that the number of reigns was quite insufficient for the purpose. It is possible that this belief was due simply to the desire of bringing the dynasty of the pious Devánampiya Tissa into immediate connexion with the founder of the Buddhist religion; it is possible also that the tradition depended partly on a fact, namely, that the colonization of Ceylon by the Aryans really took place about as long before the time of Devánampiya Tissa

[1] Mahávansa, p. 47. Dípavansa Bhánavára ix.

as the chroniclers supposed Gautama to have died. In the former case the names of Wijaya's successors may have been correctly preserved, and the numbers only be wrong; in the latter case the list of names also would be incomplete, and the record would only have preserved the memory of isolated, not consecutive, events during the period in question. This seems the more probable; but it is scarcely necessary for our argument to examine more minutely into this question here. It is sufficiently evident from the details given that the numbers at least are untrustworthy, and that the story of Wijaya himself is in great part legendary.

118. It may be suggested that, if the above conclusions as to the relation between the Rája-paramparás and the Thera-parampará be correct, the later Páli chronologists must have soon seen that the short list of six Theras was scarcely consistent with the long date which had then become part of the Ceylon chronology: and further that as they corrected the other lists of names to agree with that date, so also they would have corrected the list of Theras to bring it into harmony with the longer period. Now it is true that I can nowhere find the list given in the Dípavansa distinctly questioned, and the Mahávansa gives the same names as the Dípavansa; but it is at least curious that a corrected list is, in fact, found in the *Madurattha Vilásiní*,[1] a commentary on the Buddhavaṅsa attributed by Turnour to Buddhaghosha.[2] M. Barthelémy St.-Hilaire thinks the tone of this work not quite the same as that of the other commentaries known to be by Buddhaghosha, and concludes that the work was certainly not written by him; adding, on the authority of M. Grimblot, that it was written in a town in the Dekhan, at the mouth of the Kavéri.[3] However this may be, it is stated in the Maduratthа Vilásiní that the Buddhavaṅsa, one of the Pitaka books, was 'perpetuated' or handed down from the time of Gautama to the Council of Patna 'by the generation or unbroken succession of the Theras (*i.e.* Thera-parampará). This is the succession: Sáriputto thero, Bhaddaji, Tisso-kassa-putto, Siggawo, Moggali-putto, Sudatto, Dhammiko, Sonako, Rewato.' This list, it must be confessed, looks exceedingly like a modification of the list found in the Dípavansa; for each Thera would naturally have been ordained from 25 to 30 years before he ordained the next on the list, and an average of about 26 years for each would just make up the 236 years required by the longer chronology.

119. There is only one other question on which a few more words must be said: the question, namely, whether the shorter dates of 150 and 168 years are any more trustworthy than the longer ones of 218 and 236 years, thus found to be incorrect? In other words, were the data before the chroniclers of such a character that, even if they had not made the blunder of 68 years now so clearly evident, they *could* have drawn a right conclusion from them. In addition to what has been said above (§ 108) on this point, it will be necessary, in order to answer this question, to answer another; whether, namely, the Thera-parampará given at § 104 contains, like the Rája-parampará, any inherent impossibilities.

[1] Turnour's analysis of this commentary in the Journal of the Bengal Asiatic Society, vol. viii. p. 791 (p. 19 of the separate reprint).

[2] Ibid. p. 789, or p. 17.

[3] Journal des Savans, Janvier, 1866, p. 55.

120. Firstly, then, it should be noticed that, were the numbers at § 104 altogether lost, we should still draw the conclusion from the list of names alone that about a century and a half must have elapsed between the death of Gautama and the accession of Aṣoka. By the rules of the Order no one could be ordained until he had completed his 20th year;[1] his *upajjháya* or superior would naturally be one of the older monks, who had been ordained 30 years or more before; we have four such intervals, and have to add 16 years for the time which is said to have elapsed between Gautama's death and Dásaka's ordination, and 12 years for the interval between Mahinda's ordination and Aṣoka's accession. This would give us a total of about 148 years. If we take the somewhat similar case of a clergyman of the present day, and trace back from the bishop who ordained him to the bishop who ordained that bishop, and so on back through four steps of the ecclesiastical succession, we should find that a similar period had elapsed.[2] There is, therefore, nothing improbable in the total of 150 years.

121. Neither, with one exception, is there any inconsistency or improbability in the details of the numbers preserved to us. It will be seen that Dásaka is said to have been *upasampanno*, i.e. full member of the Order, for 50 years, and to have been only 64 when he died. This is inconsistent with the rule referred to in the last paragraph, according to which he cannot have been 14 years old when he was ordained. If we read any number below 44, say 40, for the 50 given above, this inconsistency would be remedied; and it is possible that better MSS. will show the existence of an old error in this number, as they have already enabled us to correct some of the others. Meanwhile I do not propose any alteration, and merely note the fact that this error of from 6 to 10 years is the only error in the details apparent from the evidence before us. As there is no improbability in the total, there is therefore no reason to compel us to reject it as, to a greater extent than six years, necessarily wrong.

122. By the argument above we have concluded that the date of Aṣoka's coronation must be fixed about 265 A.D. or shortly after; say certainly between 260 and 273. We have now concluded that the details given in the Dípavansa fix the death of Gautama at 140–150 years before that event. By adding the two numbers together we obtain an approximate result of between 400 and 423 B.C. (say a few years more or less than 412 B.C.) for the date of Gautama's death, according to the oldest Ceylon authorities—a result nearly as useful, for most historical purposes, as if it could be fixed to a single day.

123. This final conclusion is not without support from some of the most trustworthy of the Northern Buddhist authorities. To them Kanishka occupies the place of Aṣoka, and Kanishka's Council has the importance which the Council of Patna has for the Southerns. Some of the Tibetan books consulted by Csoma place the Council at 400 years after the Buddha's death;[3] and Hiouen Thsang, the learned Chinese Pilgrim, says that Kanishka ascended the throne about 400 A.B.[4]

[1] Upasampadá-Kammaváca, ed. Dickson, pp. 4, 10.

[2] In the list of Jain Theras, the fourth after Sudharma, himself ordained by the Mahávíra, is said to have died 146 years after Vardhamána. Stevenson's Kalpa Sútra, p. 100.

[3] Csoma Körösi, Asiatic Researches, vol. xx. pp. 92, 297. Compare J.B.A.S. vol. vii. p. 143.

[4] Stanislas Julien's translation, Mémoires sur les contrées occidentales, vol. i. p. 172.

It is acknowledged that Kanishka began to reign about the commencement of our era,[1] and he held his council some years later. These statements would therefore make the Buddhist era about 400 B.C. But the number 400 used in them is a round number, we do not know the data on which these traditions are founded, and I cannot cite them as at all conclusive.[2] I have also endeavoured to arrive at some conclusion on the basis of the Jain era, but have only been able to reach negative results of very little value. The most common date for the Jain era, dating from Vardhamána's death,[3] is 527 B.C.; but I cannot find how old this tradition is, or how early the era was used, or on what calculation it is based. I am convinced that Vardhamána and Gautama, the Buddha and the Mahávíra, are not, as some have supposed, the same person; and I do not think there is yet sufficient proof for Colebrooke's and Stevenson's opinion that Siddhártha Gautama is the same as Indrabhúti Gautama, the pupil of Vardhamána. It is only certain that the Nigaṇṭhas, a sect referred to in the Pitakas, and of which the Jains are the modern representatives, existed as early as the Buddhists; and that a complete discussion of the earliest Jain books would throw great light upon the period in which both originated.

124. SUMMARY. 1. Of the numerous dates assigned by different writers of the Northern and Southern schools, to the death of Gautama, we can only test one,—that given by the Ceylon chroniclers, which place it in 543 B.C. (§§ 83–86).

2. This date is found to be arrived at by adding to the date 161 B.C., at which the accession of Dushṭa Gámaṇi is fixed, two periods of 146 and 236 years, making together 543. The former is the period from Devánampiya Tissa, whose accession is thus placed in 307 B.C., to Dushṭa Gámaṇi; the latter is the period between the death of Gautama and the 18th year after King Aṣoka's coronation, which is the year of Devánampiya Tissa's accession (§§ 87, 88).

3. The first date, 161 B.C., is correct. But the period of 146 years is certainly too long by about 60 years; as Aṣoka's coronation can be fixed, through his own relations and those of his grandfather Chandragupta with the Greeks, at within a few years of 265 B.C. (§§ 89–97).

4. The other period of 236 years is also open to grave doubt. The successions or lists of Kings (*Rája-parampará*) in Magadha and Ceylon, which support it, are found by criticism to be untrustworthy (§§ 99–102).

5. In the oldest Ceylon Chronicle, the Dípavaṅsa, is found a list of successive Theras (*Thera-parampará*) from Gautama to Aṣoka's son Mahinda, which also seems, at first sight, to be full of incredible statements. On further examination, however, it is found to give figures, not necessarily untrustworthy, which give dates 150 A.B. for Aṣoka's coronation, and 168 A.B. for the Council of Patna and the introduction of Buddhism into Ceylon in the first year of

[1] Lassen, Indische Alterthumskunde, vol. ii. p. 848 (2nd ed.).

[2] The different Burmese eras given by Bigandet, Life of Gaudama, 2nd ed. p. 380 (comp. pp. 323, 347, 361), are calculated on the ordinary one derived from Ceylon, after the dates 218 and 236 had become fixed.

[3] Prinsep in his 'Useful Tables' gives another era, 569 B.C., which dates apparently from the time when Vardhamána became an ascetic. The possibility of some similar confusion in Buddhist computations should not be lost sight of; especially as, according to the earliest use of the word, the Buddha certainly attained Nirvána under the Bo-Tree, that is to say, 45 years before he died (see my 'Buddhism,' pp. 111, 116).

Devánampiya Tissa's reign. These figures also afford an explanation of the mistake by which the longer dates could have been reached; and enable us to harmonize the Hindu and the Ceylon lists of Kings of Magadha, while they throw unexpected light on the figures of the native list of Ceylon Kings during the same period (§§ 103–118).

6. These considerations have at least advanced the question of the Buddhist era one step nearer to solution. But they can hardly as yet be considered to do more; for it is a long step from saying that the succession of Theras is not necessarily untrustworthy, or even that it is probably correct, and saying that it is entirely conclusive. It is reasonable to hope that the publication of the three *Piṭakas*, and of the commentaries on them, will throw further light on this important point; meanwhile it is at present abundantly clear that the earliest possible date for Gautama's death is 218 years before Aṣoka's coronation, or in other words, between 478 and 491 B.C.; but that this date is very uncertain, as the details which make up this sum of 218 years are unreliable. And it is further clear that, if the Thera-paramparâ in the Dípavansa can be depended upon—which, within a few years, it probably can—the death of Gautama took place more than half a century later. In that case, by adding the period of 140–150 years to the correct date of Aṣoka's coronation, namely 260–273 B.C., we arrive at the approximate date for the commencement of the Buddhist era between 400 and 423 B.C., or say within a few years of 412 B.C. (§§ 119–123).

SUPPLEMENTARY NOTE ON THE SAHSARA'M AND RU'PNA'TH EDICT.

Just as this Part of the 'Numismata Orientalia' was on the point of being sent to press, the number of the *Indian Antiquary* for June, 1877, has come to hand, containing Dr. Bühler's learned and ingenious paper on the newly-discovered Edict, which he assigns to Aṣoka, and which he interprets as giving the number of years between the time of Gautama's death and the date of the Edict.

The Edict has been found in three places; at Sahasrám, Rúpnáth, and Bairát. It commences by saying that DEVÁNAMPIYA had been an *upásaka* for more than 32½ years without exerting himself strenuously; but that since a year and more he had entered the Society *(Saṁgha)*. Further on it quotes a saying or doctrine *(sávana)* inculcating strenuous endeavour, and states that this doctrine was preached by the *Vyuṭha* or *Vivutha;* and it then adds a number. As the texts differ slightly, I give, in full, the words of this last and most important sentence:

Sahasrám. *Iyam cha savane vivuthena duve sapaṁnálátisatá vivuthá ti* 256.[1]

Rúpnáth. *Vyuṭhena sávane kata* 256 *satavivásáta.*[2]

Dr. Bühler's rendering of the sentence from the Sahasrám text is: 'And this sermon (is) by the Departed. Two hundred (years) exceeded by fifty-six have passed since;' and of the sentence from the Rúpnáth text is: 'This sermon has been preached by the Departed; 256 (years have elapsed) since the departure of the Teacher.' The corresponding sentence in the Bairát copy is unfortunately quite illegible.

It will be seen that the whole edict taken together is quite ambiguous; each text gives the same number of years[3] as having elapsed from a certain event to the time of the edict; but while that event, in the Sahasrám text, seems to be the preaching of the doctrine referred to, in the Rúpnath text it is the 'departure of the Teacher.' The name and rank of the speaker, the nature of the religion to which he belonged, and the name of the Preacher or Teacher whose words he purports to quote, are left to be inferred. Even the figures supposed to represent the number 256 differ in the published facsimiles of the two different texts in which they occur; but this is of minor importance, for in the Sahasrám text the figures are accompanied by words which can mean nothing else.

This complete ambiguity is the more vexatious since the determination of any one of the doubtful points would enable us, with tolerable certainty, to determine the rest; and thus to obtain an authority for Indian chronology older and more authentic than any, except the Greek notices of Chandragupta, which we yet possess. It is not, therefore, a matter for surprise that eminent scholars should have been tempted, on what seem insufficient grounds, to resolve the doubt. Dr. Bühler argues that *Vyuṭha* or *Vivutha*, meaning 'the Departed,' is a name which suits the Buddha very well; that *Sata*, meaning 'the Teacher,' certainly refers to him; that *Vivása*, 'Departure,' means death; and that, therefore, the edict is dated from the death of the Buddha. Further, that *Devánam piya*, meaning 'Beloved of the Gods,' is a royal title, analogous to our 'By the grace of God,' or the Roman 'Augustus'; that we know of no Indian princes who made any great efforts for Buddhism in the third century after the Buddha's death besides Aṣoka and his grandson Daṣaratha; that it is not known that the title Devánam piya, or the alphabet of these inscriptions, were used by any one but the princes of Aṣoka's dynasty, their subjects and contemporaries; and that Daṣaratha cannot be the author of the inscriptions, as he reigned only seven years. Finally, therefore, that the edict is Aṣoka's, and that it dates the death of Buddha 256 years

[1] *Savana* is a mistake for *sávana;* and *paṁnála* for *paṁnáha* or *paṁnása.*

[2] *Vyuṭhená* is a mistake for *vyuṭhena;* and Dr. Bühler reads *kate*, that form being required to agree with *sávane.*

[3] The word years is not mentioned, which is perhaps strange; but no other substantive can be understood in both texts.

before the 34th year after Aṣoka's conversion to Buddhism; and this conversion having taken place in the 8th year of his reign, commencing between 261 and 273 B.C., the date of Gautama's death is thus fixed between 483 and 471 B.C.

If only the first three steps of the argument were indisputable, the rest would certainly follow; but, as I have already pointed out in the *Academy* of July 14th, if *Sata-vivása* is taken to be a Buddhist expression, and to stand for a suggested Páli *Satthu-vivása,* it would mean not 'the death of the Teacher' (for which *Parinibbána,* or one of its well-known synonyms, would almost certainly have been used), but 'the Teacher's abandoning his home to become an ascetic'; *vivása* thus standing for *nekkhamma.* For *vasati* means to live at a place, not in the sense of being alive there, but in the sense of dwelling there; and *vivása* would mean the going away from home, the giving up of fixed family life, that abandonment of the world which Buddhists and Brahmans alike held a necessary preliminary to the highest religious life.[1] As this step in the Buddha's career, which the Buddhists call 'the Great Renunciation,' took place in the 52nd year before his death, the edict, if really Aṣoka's, and if speaking of the Buddha as 'the Vivutha,' would place the Buddhist era between 431 and 419 B.C.

This result would be strikingly near to the conclusion reached above; but though I was at first inclined to accept, doubtfully, this interpretation of the edict as the most probably correct, I scarcely think that we can go even thus far with Dr. Bühler. For just as *parinibbána* would be the natural expression for the death of a Buddha, so *nekkhamma* or *abhinikkhamana,* and not *vivása,* would be the natural expression for the Great Renunciation; and I cannot understand why, in an edict of this kind, the usual word should have been displaced by one that may indeed exist, but has not yet been found in any of the Buddhist Sanskrit or Páli texts. And, for a similar reason, I cannot believe, without further proof, that either *Vyuṭha* or *Vivutha* would have been used instead of any of the well-known epithets of the Buddha.[2]

It is indeed true that *vyuṭha,* the past participle of *vi-vas,* to leave one's home,[3] would be an epithet very appropriate to all hermits, ascetics, or members of the Buddhist Order; but it would not be peculiarly characteristic of a Buddha; and in point of fact the epithet is not found in Páli writings, in which the idea has found another and common expression in the cognate words *anagári, anágáriya, anagárika,* and *anágára,* all meaning the houseless, homeless, one, *i.e.* an ascetic.[4] *Vivutha* is, I think, as pointed out by Professor Pischel, only another form of *vyuṭha.* Dr. Bühler indeed takes both words as forms of the past part. of *vi-vart,* to turn away from, go away from; but this does not explain the aspirate, while the confusion between the dental and the cerebral *t* s, the only objection to Dr. Pischel's explanation, is amply justified by the dental form being found in Páli as against the cerebral in Sanskrit. In Sanskrit the past participle of the simple verb being *ushita,* and *vyushita* the most common form of the p.p.p. of the compound verb, yet for the latter *vyushṭa* is also used.[5] The compound verb does not occur, or rather has not yet been found, in Páli; but the past participle of *vasati* is most commonly *vuttha,* though *vasita* and *ushita* are also found. Whilst therefore the form *vyuṭha* corresponds to the Sanskrit *vyushṭa,* the form *vivutha* corresponds to a possible Páli *vivuttha.* On the other hand, the verb *vivart* makes its past participle in Sanskrit *vivṛitta,* in Páli *vivatta* or *vivaṭṭa,* and in Jain-Prákrit *viyaṭṭa.*[6] The

[1] Stevenson, Kalpa Sútra, p. 96, reconciles two apparently inconsistent dates for the Jain era by saying, 'The date here given is founded on the mistake of the abandonment of the world for death.' Böhtlingk-Roth give as the only meaning for *vivása* in Sanskrit, 'Das verlassen der Heimat, Entfernung aus der Heimat, Verbannung (intrans.).'

[2] So also Prof. Pischel, in the *Academy,* 11th August, 1877.

[3] This is the ordinary sense, with the negative force of *vi.* It also occurs, with the intensive force of *vi,* in the sense of remaining, lingering, passing time, with the accusative of the time spent; and it is in this sense that the p.p.p. is used the second time at the end of the clause in the Sahásrám text, quoted above.

[4] The same expression is used by the Jains. Dr. S. J. Warren's 'Doctor-dissertation,' Over de Godsdienstige en Wijsgeerige Begrippen der Jainas; Zwolle, 1875; pp. 24, 69.

[5] Dr. Pischel says not; but examples of this form will be found in Böhtlingk-Roth, not only from the native dictionaries, but also from the Mahábhárata.

[6] Dr. E. Müller, Beiträge zur Grammatik des Jaina-prákrit, pp. 17, 32. Dr. S. J. Warren, De Jainas, p. 29.

point seems clear enough; but even if Dr. Bühler be right, the same argument applies, for neither *vivatta* nor *vivaṭṭa* occurs among the epithets applied by the Buddhists to their Teacher.[1]

There remains, then, of the words claimed by Dr. Bühler as Buddhist terms, only *Sata*, which he takes to be the representative of the very common Páli epithet *Satthá*, nom. case of *Satthu*, the Teacher, the Sanskrit *ṣástṛi*. This identification, however, presents great difficulties, even if it be at all possible. It is most difficult to believe that the final vowel could be a simple *a*, or that this word could appear in a form without the aspirate to replace the *s*; especially as this aspirate would be required also to distinguish the word from the corresponding forms of such common words as *sapta* and *satva*. Dr. Pischel proposes therefore to take *sata* for *satva* 'being, existence,' and to translate *sata-vivása* by 'departure from life' in the Jain sense. But this compound could never mean to depart from one life to go into another; it could only mean departure from existence altogether; and in either case the word *vivása* would be then out of place, and the idea would be not only more shortly but more correctly expressed by *nirváṇa*. For though the Jain system of philosophy cannot be discussed in the middle of this note, it is sufficiently clear that the Jain books at present accessible use *nirváṇa* in the sense of the death of a Jain saint; and that their nirvána is not a departure from existence at all, but either the absorption of the soul (in which they certainly believe) into the world-spirit, which is Dr. Warren's opinion;[2] or its entrance to a realm of bliss called Alokákása, which is Mádhava's statement,[3] and is confirmed by the author of the Nava Tatwa.[4] If, therefore, Prof. Pischel's derivation holds, it destroys his interpretation of the edict; and if *satva-vivása* is a possible expression at all, it means going out of existence, and is a Buddhist phrase.

Saṁgha, Dr. Bühler (p. 6) acknowledges to be as much a Jain as a Buddhist technical term for their Orders or Societies;[5] and it tells even against his theory, for, if Aṣoka ever did enter the Buddhist Saṁgha, it is most strange that the Buddhist monks, who have told us so much about him, should not have mentioned this important fact. On the other hand, in abandoning *upásaka* to the Jains, he perhaps passes over an argument of some force for his view of the meaning of the edict; for whilst *upásaka* is the standing expression among the Buddhists for lay-disciples, the corresponding Jain word is *ṣrávaka*.[6] But in our ignorance of Jain literature it can, perhaps, scarcely be maintained that the Jains did not use *upásaka* also; just as the Buddhists also use *sávaka*, though in a slightly different sense, as a 'true hearer' of the Word. It should be added that while the Sahasrám and Bairát texts clearly read *upásake*, the Rúpnáth text is here doubtful, Dr. Bühler reading *sa(va)ki*; but the *sa* is not clear (it looks like *su*), and the *ki* is clearly *ko*, while the injured space between is so large that two letters, and not only one, must apparently be supplied.

But if there be nothing distinctively Buddhist in the inscription, Dr. Bühler's strongest argument —that the only *Devánam piya* who, in the third century of the Buddhist era, was a zealous Buddhist and reigned more than 34 years, was no other than Aṣoka himself—does not necessarily apply to this edict, and cannot be made use of to identify our *Devánam piya* with Aṣoka. That the epithet was used of other Buddhist kings, we know from the instance of the Ceylon king Tissa; and that it must have been afterwards commonly used is sufficiently apparent from the fact that in later times in Gujarát, though it is also used as an epithet of the Mahávíra,[7] its meaning had so far deteriorated that it appears in Jain writings as a common polite address; like Sir! Madam! or Gentlemen! Thus in the *Bhagavatí* (13th century) by the Mahávíra to a disciple (Warren, p. 68); and in the *Kalpa Sútra* (6th or 7th century) by a Brahmán to his wife (Stevenson, pp. 27, 29); by her to him (*ibid.* pp. 26, 30); by King Siddhártha to his wife, the mother of the Mahávíra (*ibid.* pp. 54, 68); by the King to bráhmans (*ibid.* pp. 64,

[1] The use of *vivattacchaddo* in the prophecies drawn from the Buddha's personal appearance does not contravene this statement.

[2] De Jainas, p. 25, and comp. p. 94.

[3] Cowell's analysis in his ed. of Colebrooke's Essays, i. 450

[4] Stevenson's translation in Kalpa Sútra, p. 126.

[5] It occurs in the Ṣatruñjaya Mahâtyâm; Weber, p. 38.

[6] E.g. Weber, *loc. cit.* p. 39. Warren, De Jainas, p. 25. Comp. Stevenson, Kalpa Sútra, pp. 93, 28. Wilson, Mahâvîra Caritra (vol. i. p. 303 of collected works).

[7] In the Skandaka legend in the Bhagavatî. Warren, p. 67

68); and even to servants or messengers (*ibid.* pp. 56, 61, 76).[1] According to Prof. Kern[2] it never occurs in Sanskrit, except in the sense of foolish, idiotic; so that its meaning must have passed through a change similar to that of our words 'silly' and 'simple,' the Dutch 'onnozel,' the French 'benêt,' and the Greek 'εὐήθης.' Though, therefore, it may be granted that *Devánam piya*, at the time of the edict, was a royal title, there is no reason to believe that it was either exclusively Jain or exclusively Buddhist.

Enough has probably been said to show that the edict is not certainly and necessarily Buddhist. Dr. Pischel goes so far as to think that *Vyuṭha* or *Vivutha* is a name of the Mahávíra, the founder of the Jains; and that the prince who published this edict was a Jain, 'probably Sampadi, the grandson of Aṣoka, who, according to the Jains themselves, was a great patron of this curious sect.' In support of this view he refers to a passage in Stevenson's translation of the Kalpa Sútra (p. 95), where it is said of the Mahávíra:

'At that time he obtained emancipation, and entered on a state of freedom from passion and absence of pain. After 900 years from his departure had elapsed, and in the 80th year of the tenth hundred. this book was written, and was publicly read in the currency of the 93rd year.'

Professor Pischel, putting the words *from his departure* in italics, argues, 'Here some such word as *vivása* must be in the original.' But Professor Jacobi of Münster, whose edition of the Kalpa Sútra will appear, I hope, before Christmas in the 'Abhandlungen für die Kunde des Morgenlandes,' has been good enough to favour me with the text of the passage, which is as follows:

. . . . so siddhe buddhe mutte antagae parinivvue savvadukhappahiṇe ‖147‖. Samaṇassa bhagava Mahávírassa jáva savvadukhappahiṇassa nava vásasayáiṁ vi-ikkantáiṁ dasamassa ya vásasayassa ayaṁ asiime saṁvacchare kále gacchai | váyanantare puṇa ayaṁ teṇaue saṁvacchare kále gacchai ‖148‖.[3]

The word for 'departure' is not therefore, as Dr. Pischel supposed, *vivása*; and thus the only authority supporting his interpretation of the Edict falls to the ground. It is curious that in his note to the passage Dr. Stevenson imagines the Jain era given by Prinsep as commencing 569 B.C. to be the one here used; and to be reckoned not from the Mahávíra's death, but from the time when he abandoned the world to become an ascetic; the usual date, 527 B.C., being just 42 years later than the other, and 42 years being the time said to have elapsed between the two events. But as I cannot find that the Jains ever actually used such an era, the suggestion does not throw any light upon the, perhaps, analogous expression in the Edict.

The technical terms found in the edict not being therefore, as far as can be yet ascertained, any more common to the Jains than to the Buddhists, the argument from the improbability of a Buddhist having used terms unusual to his sect would apply with equal force to a Jain. A better acquaintance with Buddhist history may remove the difficulties which seem at present inseparable from Dr. Bühler's explanation of the edict; and a better acquaintance with Jain history may clearly show that it must be ascribed to a Jain sovereign. But for the complete and certain interpretation of this remarkable historical document we must wait till our knowledge is increased by other discoveries, or by the publication of earlier Jain texts, and of the Buddhist Pitakas.

[1] On most of the above passages from the Kalpa Sútra compare Mr. Thomas (Jainism, or the Early Faith of Aṣoka, p. 54).

[2] Jahrtelling der zuidelijke Buddhisten, p. 13.

[3] *i.e.* . . . . . 'that pure. enlightened, saved One died, past away, ceased from all sorrow. Since the Saint, the Blessed One, the Hero ceased from all sorrow, 900 years, and the 80th year in the 10th hundred, elapsed; and again, at the Recitation the 93rd year elapsed.' Unless Professor Jacobi can tell us what is referred to by the word I have rendered 'Recitation' (of which the Jain commentators give four inconsistent explanations), the chronology of this passage is provokingly vague. The Introduction to his Kalpa Sútra is to contain a full discussion of the historical questions connected with the origin of Jainism.

STEPHEN AUSTIN AND SONS, PRINTERS, HERTFORD.

INDEX.

Any matters to which this Index is not a guide will be easily found by help of the full Table of Contents. The references are to the sections, unless pages are mentioned.

A.

Abbhantara, 25
Abhidhâna-ppadípika, 4, 23
Aka and akkha = aksha, 2, 20, 23
Āḷhaka, 32, 33, 34
Ammaṇa, 31*n*., 32, 33
Angula (inch), 25, 26
Añjali, *see* Handful
Aṣoka, date of, 89–93
„ Avadâna, 4
„ Edicts, 18, 91
„ his contemporaries, 91

B.

Bambu, *see* Nâli
Bârahât bas-reliefs, 4
Bet or wager, 14
Bhuvaneka Bâhu, 44, 57
Buddhaghosha, 5, 16, 17
Buddha's span, 26*n*.
„ death, different dates of, 83, 84, 85, 122, 123, 124
Burmese eras, 123*n*.

C.

Canon of Northern Buddhists, 3
„ Southern Buddhists, 4
Ceylon history, 1
Chânakya, 19
Chandragupta, date of, 90
„ money, in time of, 19
Cholians, 35
Christian era, 86, 123
Cívara-cetâpana, 10
Coḍaganga Râja, 42, 53
Coin, meaning of the word, 5
Coins, earliest, in India, 22
Council of Kanishka, 3
„ Vesâli, 17, 18, 113
„ Patna, 4, 14, 84
Cowries, 70
Cubits of different lengths, 25, 26, 30

D.

Devânam Piya, p. 59
Devânam Piya Tissa, 88, 94, p. 59
Dhammapada, *v*. Pitaka
Dharana, 20, 23, 24
Dharmâṣoka Deva Râja, 42, 56
Dinâra, 2*n*.
Dípavansa, 84, 87, 104*n*., 108
Doṇa, 32, 33
Dutch East India Company, 75
Duṭṭha Gâmiṇi, 88, 94

E.

English Ceylon Coins, 76–81

F.

Fa Hian, 28, 85
Fanam, 79

G.

Gahâpaṇa, *see* Kahâpana
Gâvuta, 25, 27
Gokaṇṇa, 30
Guñjâ, 16, 23, 24

H.

Handful, 32, 34
Hattha, *see* Cubit
Hatthapâsa, 30
Hirañña, 8, 18
Hook money, 68

J.

Jains, 120, 123, pp. 56, 60
Jâtaka, *see* Pitaka
„ commentary, 14, 15
Justinus, 90

K.

Kâca or Kâja, 24
Kaccâyana's Grammar, 9, 33
Kahâpaṇa, 4, 5, 12, 13, 14, 17, 18, 19, 22
Kâkadvípa, 37
Kâkaṇi, 3*n*.
Kâkaṇikâ, 16
Kalanda, 20
Kalinga, 41, 42
Kâmboja, 37
Kammavâcâ, 4, 108
Kaṁsa, 12, 22
Kanakavarṇa Sûtra, 3*n*., 4
Kanishka, 3
Kankhâ Vitaraní, 12, 30
Karapuṭa, *see* Handful
Karísa, 31
Karisâpana, *see* Kahâpaṇa
Karsha, 5
Kârshâpaṇa, 3*n*., 5
Kashmír, 1
Kâṣyapa Râja, 36
Khâri, 32, 33
Kiriya, 34
Kosa, 25, 26
Knox's Ceylon, 68
Kuḍuba, *see* Handful
Kukku, *see* Cubit
Kulasekhara, 38
Kumbha, 32, 33

L.

Lacquer money, 13
Lâha, 31*n*.
Lankeṣvara, 46, 47, 48
Lari or Larin, *see* Hook money
Lead money, 15
Lílâvatí, 41, 42, 54

M.

Madurattha Vilâsiní, 118
Magadha, Kings of, 99, 110
Mahâ Vagga, *see* Pitaka
Mahâvansa, 18, 84, 108
„ Ṭíkâ, 19
Mahinda, 95, 104, 108
Maldive Islands, 70
Mâṇikâ, 32
Manu, 8, 9
Mâsa, 17
Mâsaka, 3*n*., 13, 14, 17, 22, 23, 41
Massa = mâsa, 41, 50, 51, 74
Megasthenes, 90

Moggallána, 23
Money, earliest form of in India, 5
,, made of various materials, 13, 15
,, bag of, 14

N.

Náḷi, 32, 33, 34
Nikkha, 8, 23
Nishka, *see* Nikkha
Nissanka Malla, 41, 48, 66

P.

Páda, 4, 22
Padesa, 30
Pæla, 31
Parákrama, 38, 44
Parákrama Báhu, 37–41, 48–51
Parrah, 31*n*.
Pasata, *see* Handful
Pátimokkha, 10, 11, 12, 30
Pattha, *see* Náli
Paya, 34
Phala, 23, 24
Pitaka—
1. Vinaya Pitaka
(*a*) Mahá Vagga, 4
(*b*) Párájika, 8
2. Sutta Pitaka
(*a*) Dhammapada, 5, 6
(*b*) Khuddaka Pátha, 7
(*c*) Raṭṭhapála Sutta, 8
(*d*) Játaka, 8, 14
Pliny quoted, 21
Porisa, 30
Pulastipura, 37, 38, 41, 44, 84
Púrṇa Avadána, 3*n*.

R.

Rámánya, 37
Ratana, *see* Cubit
Rati, 24
Raṭṭhapála Sutta, *see* Pitaka
Ridi, 73
Rúpiya, silver, 11

S.

Sahasrám Edict, 55
Sáhassa Malla Rája, 42, 55
Sakaṭa, 32, 33
Sanghamittá, 95
Seleukos Nikator, 90
Setu, Adam's Bridge, 62, 63
Siam, 36
Silver money in India, 11
,, ,, Ceylon, 73
Sísa, 15
Span, 25, 26, 30
Stuiver, 75, 78
Suvaṇṇa, 8, 23
Suvarṇa, 4, 8

T.

Tála, 30
Tangom, 74
Theras, Buddhist, 99–120
,, Jain, 120*n*.
Trident, 46

U.

Upajjháya, 105, 112, 120
Usabha, 25, 26

V.

Váha, 32, 33
Vardhamána, 120, 123
Vidatthi, *see* Span
Vishnu, 63
Vyáma, 30

W.

Wiyaya Báhu I., 36
,, ,, II., 40, 52
,, ,, III., 43
,, ,, IV., 44

Y.

Yála, 34
Yaṭṭhi (pole), 25
Yojana, 27, 28, 29
Yuga, 30